# Let My People Go

# LET MY PEOPLE GO

## A JOURNEY THROUGH EXODUS

## by Jack Finegan

*HARPER & ROW, PUBLISHERS*
*New York and Evanston*

FIRST EDITION

M-M

LIBRARY OF CONGRESS CATALOG CARD NUMBER: 63-7603

# CONTENTS

# PREFACE

In a previous volume entitled *In the Beginning* a journey was made through the book of Genesis. The present volume continues that journey through the book of Exodus. On any journey the manner of going is necessarily adapted to the terrain to be traversed. In Exodus we soon find ourselves in the midst of many thorny problems as to whether the Israelites were ever in Egypt and if so where they lived, how they got out, and whither they went, and whether Moses was an actual person or not and if he was what he believed, what he did, and what he taught.

With regard to such questions as these that strange dichotomy which pervades so much biblical study in our time often appears, namely, the affirmation on the one hand that we cannot possibly find out what actually happened and that it is even a misguided effort to try, and the exhortation on the other hand to share the faith of those who participated in the events now obscured from view, which remarkable but unfortunately hidden events were the very basis of their faith. Thus, as we shall quote later in our text, Martin Noth says of the exodus that "the incident itself, which the Israelites experienced as an unexpected and mighty act of deliverance of their God, remains veiled from our sight"; and James Muilenburg, to give another example, writes: "If one is tempted to raise the legitimate and necessary question, What was it that happened at the Sea of Reeds? then there is the equivocal answer that the historian is forced to give because he really does not know. There is also the answer that faith gives: 'Our God delivered us from bondage.' "[1]

The records of the event thus declared to be quite inaccessible to us, and at the same time basic to the biblical faith in which we are called to participate, do in fact, however, contain not a few references to specific places, persons, and happenings. Therefore it is the belief of the present writer that it is both proper and necessary to deal with these references as seriously as possible in the light of all obtainable information about the ancient world and time in which the event is represented as having taken place. Further, one must do this without making either the literary prejudgment that the sources are of such a sort that they cannot possibly contain useful historical information, or the theological prejudgment that it is impertinent and irrelevant to inquire after the historical bases of faith.

For this reason we are obliged to go into the details which Exodus provides about the exodus, and into the details which archeology provides about the world of that time, and, since the relevant materials are not widely known or readily accessible, to do so at sufficient length and with sufficient documentation to show the basis for the conclusions which we draw. Thus it is that the historical-archeological part of our present volume attains the proportions which it has.

But in journeying through a biblical book it is our purpose not only to study with serious historical interest the records against the background of the time and place as known from archeology, but also to ask, as I think the general reader would want to do, about the meaning of the book for theological understanding and for contemporary living. Therefore we are concerned, for example, not only about the "event" at the "Reed Sea," but also about the "theology" of Moses in his belief in YHWH, and about the "ethics" of such commandments as he may have communicated to the people who, under his leadership, were in the process of becoming a people of God. And if that people and other people too have continued to cherish a dream of human freedom which was born long ago under Egyptian slavery,[2] we shall not hesitate to suggest that the ideals of Exodus are still effective in the world and that the God of Exodus is still active in the world.

JACK FINEGAN

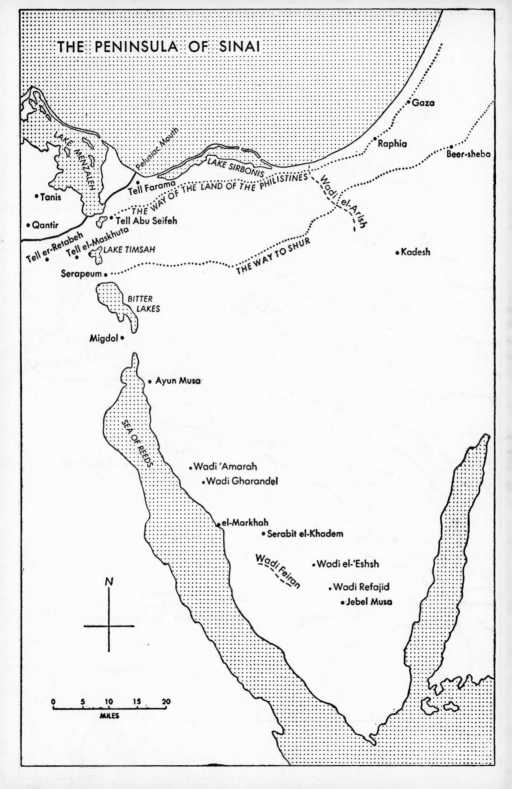

# THE PENINSULA OF SINAI

LAKE MENZALEH

Pelusiac Mouth

LAKE SIRBONIS

• Gaza

• Raphia

• Beer-sheba

• Tanis

Tell Farama •

THE WAY OF THE LAND OF THE PHILISTINES

Wadi el-Arish

• Qantir

• Tell Abu Seifeh

Tell er-Retabeh •

• Tell el-Maskhuta

LAKE TIMSAH

THE WAY TO SHUR

• Kadesh

Serapeum •

BITTER
LAKES

Migdol •

• Ayun Musa

SEA OF REEDS

• Wadi 'Amarah

• Wadi Gharandel

• el-Markhah

• Serabit el-Khadem

Wadi Feiran

• Wadi el-'Eshsh

N

• Wadi Refajid

• Jebel Musa

0    5    10    15    20

MILES

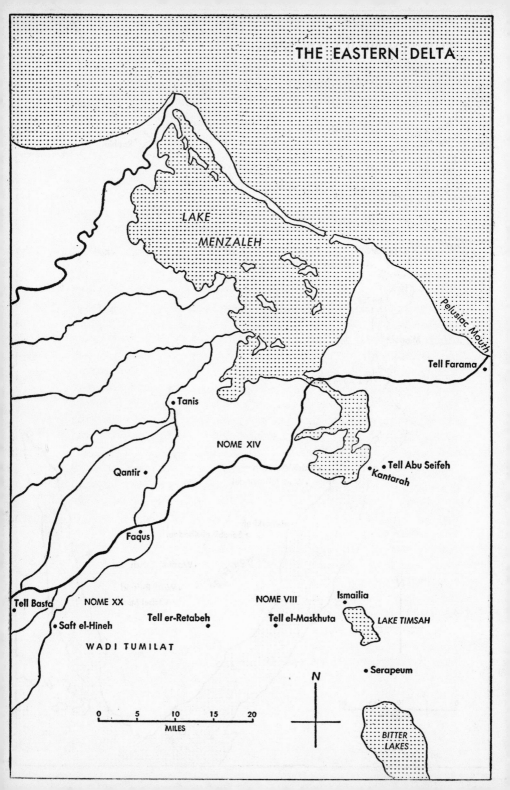

# THE EASTERN DELTA

*Pelusiac Mouth*

LAKE
MENZALEH

Tell Farama

Tanis

NOME XIV

Tell Abu Seifeh

Qantir
Kantarah

Faqus

Ismailia

Tell Basta
NOME XX
NOME VIII
LAKE TIMSAH

Saft el-Hineh
Tell er-Retabeh
Tell el-Maskhuta

WADI TUMILAT

Serapeum

N

0   5   10   15   20
MILES

BITTER
LAKES

# 1 THE HOUSE OF BONDAGE
## (Exodus 1)


At the opening of the book of Exodus the children of Israel are dwelling in the land of Egypt. What happened to them there? In working out the answer to this general question we may ask as the first of several particular questions, Who were there? for this is the very matter on which Exodus 1 provides information at the outset. The chapter begins with the words, "Now these are the names," and this phrase provides the designation of the entire book in Hebrew, We'ēleh shemôth (transliterated by Origen in Greek as Ouelesmōth), or Shemôth, "Names," for short. "Now these are the names of the children of Israel, which came into Egypt; every man and his household came with Jacob" (Exodus 1:1 KJV).

Jacob, who had received the additional name of Israel, was the aged patriarch, the grandson of Abraham. At the age of one hundred and thirty (Genesis 47:28: 147 minus 17 equals 130) he made the descent into Egypt. He had twelve sons. The eleven who went to Egypt with him are listed here, and it is explained that one, namely Joseph, was already in Egypt. Grouped according to their mothers, these sons were: the sons of Leah: Reuben, Simeon, Levi, Judah, Issachar, Zebulun; the son(s) of Rachel: (Joseph who was already in Egypt, and) Benjamin; the sons of Bilhah: Dan and Naphtali; and the sons of Zilpah: Gad and Asher.

All together it is stated that the offspring of Jacob were seventy persons. This number can be understood from the family list in Genesis 46, where all the personal names are given. Limiting ourselves for the most part to the figures, we learn that Reuben had four sons, Simeon six, Levi three, Judah five sons (two of whom, Er and Onan, actually died already in Canaan) and two grandsons,

1

Issachar four sons, and Zebulun three; so the six men with their twenty five sons and two grandsons made a total of thirty-three in the Leah group. There was also a daughter of Leah, named Dinah, but she is not counted in the initial reckoning and her name may have been a later addition in the text, since the Hebrew is awkward at this point. Joseph had two sons, born in Egypt, and Benjamin had ten, so in the Rachel group there were fourteen in all. Dan had one son, and Naphtali four which makes seven persons in the Bilhah group. Finally, Gad had seven sons, and Asher four sons, one daughter (who is counted), and two grandsons, so there were sixteen in the Zilpah group. The total of the four groups is, accordingly, seventy persons. But a different writer, whose notation we can see in Genesis 46:26-27, evidently thought that it was incorrect to count Er and Onan (since they died in Canaan) and Joseph and his two sons (since they were in Egypt already), and that it was proper to include Dinah, so he gave a figure of sixty-six; then, adding Joseph and his two sons, and Jacob himself, he too arrived at a final total of seventy. The Septuagint in turn added in Genesis 46: 20 the names of three grandsons and two great-grandsons of Joseph, and therefore says (verse 27) that the total in Egypt was seventy-five. Stephen the Hellenist doubtless read his scriptures in the Greek and, in his address in Acts 7:14, he stated that it was seventy-five souls who were in Egypt. Exodus 1:5, however, evidently follows the list as we worked through it first above and gives the offspring of Jacob as numbering seventy persons.

These were the children of Israel who were in Egypt. After seventeen years (Genesis 47:28) Jacob died. Then (Exodus 1:6) Joseph died, and all of his brothers, and all of that generation. But their descendants lived on in Egypt through succeeding generations, and multiplied in numbers. To them all we give the name, the children of Israel.

Why had they come to Egypt? is a question to which the answer has already been provided in the story of Joseph in the book of Genesis. In brief and at its most essential point, the answer lies in the fact that there was famine in the earth and there was food in Egypt. Here we need to notice only that for people to come into Egypt under such circumstances happened many times in Egyptian history. There is a striking illustration in the tomb of Haremhab. This man was a general who was associated with the famous king, Akhenaton, and later, at the end of the Eighteenth Dynasty, somewhat before 1300 B.C., himself became king of Egypt. His tomb, built of limestone, was at Saqqara, and the fragments of its reliefs and inscriptions are now scattered in half a dozen different museums. On a block of stone which was taken to Vienna, there is a carving which shows a group of Egyptian officials bowing before Haremhab (whose own picture is actually missing), as he gives them instructions on what to do with certain Asians.[1] The Asians have come to Egypt, the inscription states, because their town has been laid waste and their countries are starving. So they beg of Pharaoh a home in Egypt, as they say, "after the manner of your fathers' fathers since the beginning." Although the picture of the Asians themselves has been destroyed, the further inscription is preserved in which they give praise to Pharaoh; therefore, it is evident that their request has been granted. In its final form the monument represents Haremhab as king, but when it was first executed he was probably shown only as general; therefore, the original construction of the tomb and the arrival of the Asians was probably under the immediate successors of Akhenaton. So at this time, and even long before, it was a familiar enough happening for people to come in from the Asiatic regions in the northeast, pressed by hunger, seeking sustenance and security in the great valley of the Nile.

Another illustration of the same situation is found in the Papyrus Anastasi VI, now in the British Museum, a document from the late Nineteenth Dynasty and the end of the thirteenth century B.C. This contains a copy of the report of a frontier official as follows:

We] have finished letting the Bedouin tribes of Edom pass the Fortress [of] Merneptah . . . which is (in) Tjeku, to the pools of Per-Atum [of] Mer[ne]ptah . . . which are (in) Tjeku, to keep them alive and to keep their cattle alive. . . .[2]

A not too different report might have been prepared when Jacob and his household came across the border of Egypt.

Where in Egypt did the children of Israel live? When Joseph asked his brothers to bring Jacob to Egypt, he said that they would dwell in the land of Goshen (Genesis 45:10); when he drove out in his chariot to meet them upon their arrival he went to Goshen (Genesis 46:28-29); while they waited for Pharaoh to say where they should go they remained in the land of Goshen (Genesis 47:1); and when the king made disposition concerning them he allowed them to settle in the land of Goshen (Genesis 47:6). From Genesis 46:32-34 it is evident that this area was specially suitable for them as shepherds with flocks and herds; from this point of view it may have been for them "the best of the land" (Genesis 47:6), although these words may also reflect the polite phraseology of Pharaoh. In Genesis 47:11 the region is called the land of Rameses and is again described as the best of the land. From the facts that the land of Goshen was where the household of Jacob arrived as they came from Canaan, that it was where they stayed while awaiting word from Pharaoh, and that it was where they were settled in view of their needs as shepherds, we gather that it was a frontier region somewhere on the east of the Delta, lying probably between the intensively cultivated river lands and the desert.

Geographically, there are two strips of fertile land which extend from the Delta toward the eastern border of Egypt, and from the earliest times these have provided natural routes of ingress and egress. One was the valley of the so-called Pelusiac branch of the Nile which flowed to the northeast and entered the Mediterranean near Pelusium, which was probably at Tell Farama near the coast east of Port Said. The other was the Wadi Tumilat. This is a long valley which begins a dozen miles southeast of Zagazig (forty miles northeast of Cairo) and extends more than thirty miles eastward to Ismailia on Lake Timsah or Crocodile Lake. The valley itself is at best scarcely a half dozen miles in width, and is bounded by the tawny hills of the desert on either side.

In ancient times a canal was dug from the Nile near Bubastis (Tell Basta, a mile and a half southeast of Zagazig) through this valley to the Bitter Lakes south of Lake Timsah and on to the Gulf of Suez. Strabo (XVII, i, 25 [804]) and Aristotle (Meteorologica I, xiv, 352b) state that the canal was begun by Sesostris. This is a royal name in the Twelfth Dynasty (Middle Kingdom), according to Manetho (it is now usually rendered as Senusert), but it seems unlikely that the canal can be placed as early as the Twelfth Dynasty. It was surely not in existence when Senusert I came to the throne. According to a well-known account found in late Twelfth Dynasty manuscripts, a certain man named Sinuhe left Egypt at this time, and probably departed by way of the Wadi Tumilat. He went, it is reported, by the Red Mountain, which must be Jebel el-Ahmar northeast of Cairo; slipped past the Wall of the Ruler, meaning the Egyptian frontier fortresses; and halted at Kem-wer, literally "the great black," probably the Bitter Lakes or in that area.[3] Since he arrived at the last point perishing from thirst, he could not have been paralleling any active fresh-water canal. Likewise, various Middle Kingdom inscriptions speak of overland transport through the Wadi Hammamat (much farther south) as the usual way of getting to the Red Sea at that time.[4] In the Greek writers generally, however, the name Sesostris seems to have attained a sort of legendary character and to embody memories most of all of the reign of Ramses II and perhaps also of Seti I, his father, with whom he was early coregent; applying this interpretation to the statements of Strabo and Aristotle, we would conclude that the canal was dug by these Nineteenth Dynasty kings.[5]

But there is other evidence which makes it more probable, we believe, that the canal was in existence already under the famous Eighteenth Dynasty queen, Hatshepsut, and might even have been dug by her. On the walls of her terraced temple at Deir el-Bahri is carved the record of a sea expedition which she sent to Punt (in Africa, probably the Somali coast), which returned, according to the only date given, in her ninth year.[6] She was commanded by the god Amon, according to this record, "that the ways to Punt should be searched out."[7] Five large ships then sailed to Punt, carrying jewelry and tools made in Egypt, and returned with incense trees, myrrh, ivory, and monkeys from the exotic land.[8] Since the same ships that are shown being loaded on the coast of Punt are afterward pictured on the Nile ("sailing, arriving in peace, journeying to Thebes" [therefore upon the Nile]),[9] they must have gone all the way by water, and the only possible way would have been by the canal through Wadi Tumilat.

Later, according to Diodorus (I, 33) and Herodotus (II, 158), work was done on the canal by Pharaoh Necho and the Persian king Darius I. During the excavation of the modern Suez Canal, one of the large granite stelae with which Darius commemorated his work was found. On it the king said in a trilingual (Old Persian, Elamite, Akkadian) inscription: "I ordered this canal to be dug from the river Nile by name, which flows in Egypt, to the sea which goes from Persia. Afterward this canal was dug thus as I commanded, and ships went from Egypt through this canal to Persia thus as was my desire."[10]

In the nineteenth century a fresh-water canal was dug from the Nile via Ismailia to Suez to supply water for the workers on the Suez maritime canal, and it followed much the same route as the ancient canal through the Wadi Tumilat. The modern railroad from Zagazig to Ismailia also goes through the same valley. This long

continued use of the route enables us to recognize, therefore, that
Wadi Tumilat was from early to late times a natural frontier passageway.

As to conditions in the valley, we have supposed that the canal
was in existence from the Eighteenth Dynasty; but as far as is
known there are not many ancient monuments from earlier than
the Nineteenth Dynasty and the reign of Ramses II.[11] Prior to
Ramses II, therefore, the Wadi Tumilat was not only a route to
and from the frontier but also itself a frontier region, such as we
have assumed above that the land of Goshen must have been,
suitable for the settlement of people with flocks and herds. Some
idea of the possibilities for settlement in this region may be obtained
from the facts that in the early nineteenth century A.D. some four
thousand Bedouins lived in Wadi Tumilat; with the modern fresh-
water canal and the practice of irrigation, the population increased
to more than twelve thousand in the early twentieth century.[12]

Not only does Wadi Tumilat correspond in general with the
character which we must assume for the land of Goshen; there are
also specific indications which point to the identification of the
two. In Genesis 45:10 and 46:34, where the settlement of the household of Jacob in Egypt is described, the Hebrew text states that it
was "in the land of Goshen," but the Septuagint version, the Greek
translation made in Egypt, reads "in the land of Gesem of Arabia."
In Genesis 46:28-29, where the meeting of Joseph with his father
is related, the Hebrew text states that Jacob sent Judah before
him to Joseph "to direct his face unto Goshen" (probably meaning
"to get instructions from Joseph about Goshen" [Moffatt]), and that
"they came into the land of Goshen. And Joseph made ready his
chariot, and went up to meet Israel his father, to Goshen" (KJV).
For this the Greek translation has: "And he sent Judah before him
to Joseph to [come to] meet him to [or, at] Heroonpolis into the
land of Ramesses. And Joseph, having yoked his chariots, went up
to meet Israel his father to [or, at] Heroonpolis." In Genesis 47:6
the Septuagint omits "the land of Goshen"; in Genesis 47:11 this
version retains "the land of Ramesses" which is also in the Hebrew.
Given the building work of Ramses II in Wadi Tumilat, referred to
in the paragraph above, it is probably not surprising than an alternate designation of this region, or of a larger area including this
region, could be "the land of Ramses." Requiring further notice are
the facts that "the land of Goshen" is rendered "the land of Gesem

of Arabia" in two passages, and "Goshen" is replaced by Heroonpolis
in one passage.

The Greek word "Gesem" seems obviously a variant of the
Hebrew "Goshen," and a possible origin of both in an Egyptian
word will be noted a little later. As for "Arabia," we know that
until today the desert which bounds the Nile Valley and the Delta
immediately on the east is called the Arabian Desert. Therefore,
we might expect "Arabia" to be used generally of the eastern border
of Egypt, and this seems to be the way in which it is used by
Strabo (XVII, i, 21 [803]) when he speaks of Pelusium "in Arabia."
But Arabia was also specifically the name of an Egyptian nome or
administrative district.

For the division of Egypt into such districts there is evidence as
early as the Pyramid Texts of the Old Kingdom, and there are lists
of the nomes in the New Kingdom (Eighteenth to Twentieth
Dynasties) and on down in Ptolemaic and Roman times. The
hieroglyphic sign for such a district is five vertical lines crossed by
three horizontal lines, doubtless signifying a net of canals; the
Greek name is *nomos* from which we derive the designation, nome.
The usual reckoning was twenty-two such districts in Upper Egypt,
twenty or more in Lower Egypt; and it goes without saying that the
boundaries as well as the numbers must have varied somewhat
from time to time.[13]

Individual nomes were known by a name as well as a number,
and the name could be determined by the location of the nome.
Thus Nome VII was west of the Delta and the westernmost (or
Canopic) arm of the Nile. It probably lay west of the Mareotic
district and north of the Oasis of Siwah, and included Paraitonion
(Mirsa Matruh) on the coast. Since it was adjacent to the Libyan
desert it was known as the Nome Libya.[14] Balancing this, Nome XX
was east of the Delta and the easternmost (or Pelusiac) arm of the
Nile. Since it was adjacent to the Arabian desert it was known as
the Nome Arabia.[15] Herodotus (II, 158) may refer to the latter
nome when he tells about the Pharaonic canal which left the Nile
a little above Bubastis and went "by the Arabian town of Patumus"
and led into the Red Sea. Strabo (XVII, i, 26 [804]) says that the
canal to the Red Sea "begins at the village Phaccusa," and Ptolemy[16]
lists the nome of Arabia and gives Phakusa as its metropolis.

The name Phakusa seems obviously preserved in the city of Faqus
(twenty miles northeast of Zagazig), but this must be the result of a
migration of the name, since the terrain would not allow a canal to

start for the Red Sea from that vicinity. The ancient capital was in fact most probably at Saft el-Hineh, which is a village on the site of an ancient city about eight miles southeast of Zagazig and just west of the entrance to the Wadi Tumilat, a location which is in the correct relation to the route of the canal as described by Strabo. The ancient name of this city was almost certainly Per-Sopd, which means "House of Sopd." The name occurs on the stela of Piankhi of the Twenty-third Dynasty as the residence of a Delta prince;[17] it is mentioned by Ashurbanipal as Pi-Shaptu;[18] and it has evidently survived in the village name of Saft. In the excavation at Saft el-Hineh by Edouard Naville,[19] in addition to a colossal statue in black granite of Ramses II, the most important monument was a great shrine, probably built by Nectanebo II of the Thirtieth Dynasty, with numerous inscriptions to the god Sopd. In these inscriptions the place where the shrine was erected is twice named *Kes*. With the article this would give *Pa Kes*, which could explain the Greek name Phakusa for the capital of the nome. Also the name *Kesem* or *Qesem* is found in other Egyptian inscriptions, both with the determinative of a land and with the determinative of a city. In one list a god appears who bears on his head the name of Sopd and of whom it is said: "He brings thee Kesem of the East."[20] If this Kesem was the Egyptian name of this region it would account for the origin of the Hebrew word Goshen and the Greek Gesem.

Thus far it has been established, therefore, that the land of Goshen was probably more or less the same as Nome XX, Arabia, of which the capital was at Per-Sopd, the present Saft el-Hineh, known to the Greeks as Phakusa. Since Nome XVIII,[21] of which Bubastis (Tell Basta, one and one-half miles southeast of Zagazig)[22] was the capital, began only a short distance to the west, the territory of Nome XX (Arabia) must have extended to the east into and perhaps through the Wadi Tumilat.

This conclusion about the location of this nome is confirmed by the character of the deity who was its chief god and after whom its capital was named. In origin Sopd (Sept, Soped, Sopdu) may have been a sun god, since he was sometimes united with Horus as Har-Sopd or Horus-Soped and, like Horus, was depicted by a falcon, in this case a falcon with plumes on his head.[23] But in his most distinctive character and as he was worshiped at Per-Sopd and in the nome of Arabia, Sopd was known as "the lord of the East." The name of Sopd, accompanied by this title, occurs repeatedly in the inscriptions of the shrine at Saft el-Hineh; it is found on a statue of around the Twenty-second Dynasty at Tell el-Maskhuta in the eastern part of Wadi Tumilat; and it also appears in a Twelfth Dynasty inscription in Wadi Maghara in the peninsula of Sinai.[24] These examples show how great, how early, and how widespread was the significance of Sopd as "the lord of the East."

The other Egyptian god who has the title "lord of the East" is Min,[25] who was worshiped far to the south at Koptos. Here the Nile bends farthest to the east and nearest to the Red Sea, and from here caravans departed to proceed through Wadi Hammamat to the sea. As the two lords "of the East," therefore, Min and Sopd were worshiped at the two cult places from which the normal routes to the east departed, namely, from Koptos through Wadi Hammamat to the Red Sea, and from Per-Sopd through Wadi Tumilat to the peninsula of Sinai. An inscription on the shrine at Saft el-Hineh also speaks of "Sopd who slays the Menziu," and since the latter were evidently Asians and are mentioned as early as in a Fifth Dynasty inscription in Wadi Maghara, this appellation points likewise to Sopd as a warlike deity of the eastern frontier.[26] Relation to the east is also indicated by frequent mention of Sopd along with the goddess Hathor who was recognized, for example in inscriptions in Wadi Maghara and at Serabit el-Khadem, as "mistress of the turquoise (mafaket) land" of Sinai.[27]

The applicability of the name Arabia to the eastern border of Egypt in general, the location of the capital city, Per-Sopd, and the character of its god as "lord of the East," all point, therefore, to the recognition that the nome Arabia was on the eastern border of Egypt and included part or all of the Wadi Tumilat, the great frontier passageway between the Delta and the peninsula of Sinai.

From the facts stated above we assume that Nome XX Arabia originally extended east to whatever point was recognized as the border of Egypt. Later it appears that the very easternmost region was recognized as constituting Nome VIII or the eastern Harpoon Nome.[28] Whether this represented a pushing of the border eastward to include additional territory, or simply the establishment of a separate administrative district in the eastern part of what had previously been Arabia, is difficult to make out. A Harpoon Nome appears at least as early as in the Third Dynasty;[29] then in a list of Amenhotep III and later lists there are distinguished a western and an eastern Harpoon Nome; and in lists of the Ptolemaic period which, of course, contain older material, the capital of the eastern Harpoon Nome is given as Pithom.[30]

The name Pithom ("House of Tum") is plainly the same as the Per-Atum ("House of Atum") to which the border official cited above (Papyrus Anastasi VI) reported letting the Edomite Bedouins go to get water, a place which was there stated to be in Tjeku. As to the god Tum or Atum, he was a form of the sun god who was worshiped particularly at the city of On, which the Greeks called Heliopolis, just north of present Cairo. We have seen that as a smiter of the Asians, the warlike Sopd was of a character appropriate to a god of the eastern Egyptian frontier. Atum, however, is originally quite lacking in such a character. His home at Heliopolis was far from the border; there he was accounted, as Sixth Dynasty texts tell us, the creator and, as such, the first of the nine gods who comprised "the Great Ennead which is in Heliopolis";[31] and always he was remembered, as in a text of Seti I of the Nineteenth Dynasty, as the "lord of Heliopolis."[32] Therefore, it must have been only secondarily that he became a god of the eastern frontier. And there, although once given the appellation "at the gate of the East," he is regularly titled simply "lord of Tjeku."[33]

This, then, is also in accord with the supposition that Nome VIII, the eastern Harpoon Nome, was established at a relatively late date, perhaps at the time when Ramses II was doing the building work in the eastern area which we have referred to above. At all events a Harpoon Nome adjacent to Crocodile Lake was appropriately named, since the harpoon served specially for the taking of the crocodile.

Given the existence of the two nomes, XX (Arabia) and VIII (eastern Harpoon), we may conclude that they corresponded respectively to the western and the eastern parts of the Wadi Tumilat.[34] As for Pithom, given the complicated relationships we have deduced, it might well have been referred to variously, either as belonging to the nome Arabia, as we saw above that Herodotus (II, 158) probably did when he spoke of the canal which went "by the Arabian town of Patumus [presumably to be identified with Pithom]," or as belonging to and indeed being the capital of Nome VIII, as we have just seen. As for the connection of the god Tum or Atum with the valley under consideration, once that connection was established it was lasting, for the present Arabic name, Tumilat, means the Valley of Tum.

The conclusion thus far is that the great eastern frontier valley, the Wadi Tumilat, provides a likely location for the biblical land of Goshen, and that the Septuagint rendering, "Gesem of Arabia,"

definitely indicates this localization. Next we have to consider the
occurrence of "Heroonpolis" in the Greek version of Genesis 46:
28-29. Here, it will be remembered, where the Hebrew speaks of
"Goshen" and "into the land of Goshen," the Greek reads, "to
Heroonpolis into the land of Ramesses"; and where the Hebrew has
"to meet Israel his father, to Goshen," the Greek reads, "to meet
Israel his father to Heroonpolis." In the same passage it is also to
be noted that the Sahidic version of Upper Egypt retains Heroonpolis in both of its occurrences, but the Bohairic version of Lower
Egypt replaces it both times with Pethōm (which must be the same
as Pithom), and reads "to the town of Pethōm in the land of
Ramassē" and "towards the town of Pethōm."[35] These facts seem to
indicate in the first place that the land of Goshen and the land of
Ramesses are the same, as we have already surmised; and in the
second place that the Hebrew Goshen is the name of a particular
town as well as of an area and that this town was known in Egyptian
as Pithom and in Greek as Heroonpolis.

There is a mention of the Heroonpolite Nome in the Egyptian
Book of the Dead,[36] and we may presume that this was a reference
to our Nome VIII. As it stands, the Greek name Herōōn Polis means
City of Heroes, but the original spelling and meaning may have been
different, for, in place of Heroon, the variants Eron, Ero, and Hero
are attested.[37] Ammianus Marcellinus (XVII, iv, 18), following
Hermapion (who probably lived in the time of Augustus), translated into Greek the inscription on a large obelisk which was
brought from Thebes and set up in the Circus Maximus at Rome
(moved in A.D. 1588 to the Lateran) as beginning: "The Sun [Helios]
speaks to King Ramestes [Ramses II]. I have granted to thee that
thou shouldst with joy rule over the whole earth, thou whom the
Sun loveth—and powerful Apollo, lover of truth, son of Herōn, god-
born, creator of the world, whom the Sun hath chosen, the doughty
son of Mars, King Ramestes. Unto him the whole earth is made subject through his valour and boldness. King Ramestes, eternal child
of the Sun."

According to this, Ramses II was the son of the Sun and the son
of Herōn. That the Egyptian king was the son of the sun god is, of
course, a very ancient doctrine. Now the solar deity, Atum, was
always associated with the kingship: he is mentioned, for example,
on a stela from Abydos as the begetter of Thutmose I and in the
Papyrus Harris as the father of Ramses III; and Atum's successor at
Heliopolis, Re, "became the father of all mortal kings of Egypt."[38]

Since in the inscription above, the Sun (Helios) and Herōn seem to
stand in parallel, it is well possible that the latter was a name of the
sun god, perhaps of Atum himself. In that case the name of our
city may properly have been Herōn Polis, Heronpolis, "City of
Heron," and this may have been a direct translation of Per-Atum,
Pithom, "House of Atum." From that, other forms such as Heropolis
and, in Latin, Ero, might easily have been derived. It appears, therefore, that the identification by the Bohairic version of the Heroonpolis of the Septuagint with Pethōm, i.e., Pithom, is fully justified.

Since Per-Sopd was the capital of Nome XX, and Per-Atum
(Pithom) the capital of Nome VIII, and these nomes corresponded
to Wadi Tumilat west and east respectively, we must look in the eastern part of Wadi Tumilat for the city of Pithom; but since Herodotus
(II, 158) could also speak of Pithom as an Arabian town, it must
have been in territory which at least some time belonged to the nome
Arabia, and therefore it would be more likely that it was in the
western part of the eastern portion of the Wadi. In the eastern half
of Wadi Tumilat there are two major ancient sites. The first is Tell
er-Retabeh (or Tell Artabi), some twenty-one miles east of Saft
el-Hineh. The second is Tell el-Maskhuta, eight and one-half miles
east of Tell er-Retabeh. From Tell el-Maskhuta it is another nine and
one-half miles on to the eastern end of Wadi Tumilat and Lake
Timsah. Tell el-Maskhuta was excavated in 1883 by Edouard
Naville,[39] who believed that this was Pithom. But a Roman milestone
found there has the Latin inscription: AB ERO IN CLVSMA
VIIII,[40] which probably means, "Nine miles on the road from Ero
to Clysma."[41] Clysma was near Suez; hence this milestone marked
a point nine miles eastward from Ero, and that places Ero almost
exactly at Tell er-Retabeh. Tell er-Retabeh may be accepted, therefore, as the probable site of Ero which, as we have already seen,
was the same as Heronpolis and Pithom.

No thorough excavation of Tell er-Retabeh has been conducted,
but in a brief exploration W. M. Flinders Petrie[42] found stone vases
of the Old Kingdom and a weight and scarabs of the Ninth to
Twelfth Dynasties, which led him to call this the oldest site known
east of Bubastis. The first fortifications were of gray brick and black
brick; a child burial beside the wall appeared to be a foundation
sacrifice which suggested Asian rather than Egyptian custom. Later
an outer brick wall was built by Ramses III of the Twentieth
Dynasty. A large house was found, containing scarabs of the Eighteenth Dynasty, and a temple of Ramses II. The temple had been

brilliantly painted in red, blue, and yellow, and was of special
interest for a relief sculptured on the front which shows Ramses II
smiting an Asian in the presence of a god who is identified in the
accompanying label as "Tum, lord of Thu."[43] Tum is of course the
god Atum, and Thu should undoubtedly be Theku, a name found
on other of the temple fragments.[44] There were also two statues
carved in a block of red granite, believed to be Ramses II and Atum,
with an accompanying inscription speaking of the work of Ramses
II in "building in cities upon which his name is to eternity."[45] The
prominence of Atum and the building work of Ramses II here are
well in accord with our identification of Tell er-Retabeh as probably
the ancient Per-Atum or Pithom. As for the name Theku (also Tjeku,
Teku, etc.), it must be spoken of further in connection with Tell
el-Maskhuta.

Tell el-Maskhuta, we recall, is eight and one-half miles east of
Tell er-Retabeh in Wadi Tumilat, and was excavated by Edouard
Naville.[39] The hieroglyphic inscriptions found here make frequent
reference to Atum and to Theku. The following are a few examples:
A fragment which preserves part of the name of Ramses II contains
also the words "the lord of Thuku." A statue of around the Twenty-
second Dynasty mentions "all the priests who go into the temple of
Tum, the great living god in the midst of Theku." A Saite fragment
names an "official of the temple of Tum of Theku." A stela of
Ptolemy II Philadelphus was erected "in front of Tum, the great
living god of Theku," and describes the return of the gods from
Persia, saying that "the gods of Pithom and Theku came to rest
there."[46] This frequent mention of Theku at Tell el-Maskhuta makes
it seem possible that Theku was the name of this particular place; if
so, the mention of both Pithom and Theku in the immediately preceding quotation suggests that Pithom and Theku were two separate
places. At the same time the frontier report found in Papyrus
Anastasi VI, quoted near the beginning of this chapter, used the
name Theku (Tjeku) as most evidently the designation of a region,
since it spoke of the pools of Per-Atum which were in Theku and
of the fortress of Merneptah which was in Theku. Perhaps both
things are true. Perhaps Theku was the name of the town at Tell
el-Maskhuta and also the name of the region in which this town
and also Pithom and other places were located. This is to say that
it was the name of the region roughly identical with the eastern
part of Wadi Tumilat.

Another observation of importance may be made concerning

Theku. This name may be the same as the biblical Succoth. At first sight it appears unlikely that there would be any direct derivation of the one word from the other. But the following facts may be noted: The name Theku or Tjeku would be written in Egyptian *T* k w. The Egyptian *t* or tj is ordinarily reproduced by the Hebrew Samekh or s; the Egyptian k of course becomes the Hebrew Kaph or k; thus we have the first two letters of Hebrew Sukkoth or Succoth.[47] The Hebrew word Succoth means "booths" and is still used as the name of the Jewish festival of booths or tabernacles at which it is recalled how the earlier Israelites dwelt at harvest time or in the wilderness in such temporary lodgings. One wonders if the Egyptian *T* k w might have had any related meaning, and there is, in fact, some evidence that the Egyptian word did have something to do with the life of nomads.[48] If this is the case, it could explain why this name was attached to the eastern part of Wadi Tumilat since, as we saw, this was the region where nomads often entered Egypt.

It may also be recalled that the frontier official's report in Papyrus Anastasi VI mentioned not only the pools of Per-Atum which were in Theku (which site, Per-Atum, we have now identified with Tell er-Retabeh), but also the fortress of Merneptah which was in Theku. It is therefore a natural question whether this fortress might be identified with Tell er-Maskhuta. The fortress should have been on the border, however, since it was the point at which the Bedouins were first admitted to Egyptian territory. We have already noted that the Egyptian word Kem-wer, which occurs in the story of Sinuhe and means literally "the great black," was probably a designation of what we know as the Bitter Lakes, half a dozen miles south of Lake Timsah. Already in the Pyramid Texts, Kem-wer occurs and is written with the determinative for a fortification.[49] Therefore, it seems likely that in the vicinity of the Bitter Lakes there was from an early time a border fortification. And in fact, in 1929 when the modern Suez Canal was being enlarged, at a site known as Serapeum between Lake Timsah and the Bitter Lakes, ancient ruins were found with a cartouche of Ramses II and an inscription saying, "The king fortifies the mouth of the canal of Theku."[50] This was no doubt one of a series of fortresses which followed the general line of the modern Suez Canal and constituted "the Wall of the Ruler" mentioned in the story of Sinuhe and other Egyptian documents.[51] The fortress just described, which could well have been known by the name of Merneptah in the time of that king, would have commanded access to the Wadi Tumilat and therefore could have been the "fortress . . . in Theku" of the frontier official's report.

Coming from the east, then, we believe that travelers would have passed the fortress between the Bitter Lakes and Lake Timsah, would have entered the Wadi Tumilat on the west side of Lake Timsah, and would have gone on past the places now marked by Tell el-Maskhuta and Tell er-Retabeh. This eastern part of Wadi Tumilat was known as Theku, and Tell el-Maskhuta may have been a particular place of that name. Later this eastern part of the valley was made Nome VIII, the eastern Harpoon Nome. Tell er-Retabeh was the Per-Atum or Pithom where the god Atum was specially worshipped, this god being considered the "lord of Theku." West of Nome VIII was Nome XX which, before Nome VIII was established, had probably itself extended all the way to the eastern border. As the border district it was known as the nome Arabia, and its god Sopd, worshiped at the capital, Per-Sopd, was the warlike "lord of the East." This region was also known as Kesem, from which was derived the name of Goshen. It was at Pithom, called Heronpolis in Greek, that Joseph met his father, Jacob, and it was in the land of Goshen, called Gesem of Arabia in Greek, that the household of Jacob was allowed to settle.

How long were the children of Israel in Egypt? Since in the case of a prison sentence one of the most important things about it is the duration, and since the Israelites ever afterward looked back upon their time in Egypt as a period of bondage, one of the most important questions about the experience would be how long it lasted. On this question, the Bible provides the following data: In Genesis 15:12-16 the Lord tells Abraham, in a deep sleep, what will happen to his descendants. They will be sojourners in a land that is not theirs, will be slaves there, and will be oppressed "for four hundred years." At this point the number four hundred is found in both the Hebrew text and the Greek translation. It is also quoted, doubtless from the Greek, by Stephen in Acts 7:6. The same number of four hundred years for the period in Egypt is also given by Josephus in two passages.[52] In Exodus 12:40 a figure of about the same magnitude but of apparently greater precision is given when it is stated that the time the Israelites dwelt in Egypt was "four hundred and thirty years."

In each of the two passages just cited there is additional and different evidence, however, which must also be considered. In Genesis 15:12-16 where God tells Abraham that his descendants will sojourn in a land not theirs for four hundred years, he also assures the patriarch: "And they shall come back here in the fourth generation." That the children of Israel did in fact return from Egypt to Canaan in the fourth generation is verified by the actual genealogies. The keeping of such family records was considered important, we know, by the Jewish people; and the record we are interested in first is that of the family of Levi who, with their hereditary rights and duties relative to the tabernacle and temple, would have been specially interested in keeping their genealogy as carefully as possible. Tracing the record just referred to as it appears in Exodus 6:16-20 and Numbers 26:57-59, we find that Levi was the son of Jacob, hence representing the first generation; Kohath was the son of Levi and was thus of the second generation; Amram was the son of Kohath and accordingly marked the third generation; and Aaron and Moses, who participated in the exodus, were the sons of Amram and so were in fact of the fourth generation.

A second totally different and independent genealogy confirms the results just reached. In Joshua 7:1 we have this line of descent from Jacob: Judah (first generation), Zerah (second generation), Zabdi (third generation), Carmi (fourth generation), and Achan (fifth generation). As the context shows, Achan, a member of the fifth generation from Jacob, was a contemporary of Joshua and, since Joshua was the successor of Moses, this too points to the generation of Moses and of the exodus as the fourth.

If it is in fact the case that the exodus was made "in the fourth generation," this very fact could account for the appearance of the number of "four hundred years." According to Genesis 21:5, Abraham was one hundred years old when his son Isaac was born; from that, some writer might easily have reckoned that four generations would be four hundred years. Actually, however, four generations must have covered a much shorter period than that. If the entire series of figures found in Genesis 12:4, 21:5, 25:26, and 47:9 be considered, it will be seen that from the time Abraham came to Canaan to the time his grandson Jacob went down into Egypt with his own sons and grandsons (which is also a period reaching into the fourth generation), there was a total of two hundred and fifteen years. Some such span as this would seem to be much more likely for the period from the descent of Jacob into Egypt to the exodus from that land of his descendants in the fourth generation. And that brings us to the additional and different evidence to be found in the second passage, Exodus 12:40.

In Exodus 12:40 the Hebrew text states that "the time that the people of Israel dwelt in Egypt was four hundred and thirty years," but the Septuagint reads that the sojourning of the children of Israel "in the land of Egypt and the land of Canaan was four hundred and thirty years." Since we have just established that the time of the patriarchs in Canaan was two hundred and fifteen years (and the same figures are given in the Greek version as in the Hebrew of Genesis 12:4, 21:5, 25:26, and 47:9), this obviously allows the Israelites only another two hundred and fifteen years in Egypt. This text is also followed by Paul, who no doubt read it in the Greek, when he says in Galatians 3:17 that the law was given to Moses four hundred and thirty years after the covenant was made with Abraham. Likewise it is followed by Josephus in one passage (which contradicts his other two cited above) in which he says that the children of Israel left Egypt four hundred and thirty years after Abraham came to Canaan and two hundred and fifteen years after Jacob came to Egypt.[53]

While it is already obvious that there are many problems in relation to such figures as these in the text, it also seems evident that such a figure as this of two hundred and fifteen years in Egypt which allows only a little more than fifty years to a generation, is at least much more like what we should expect than the figure of four hundred or four hundred and thirty years. Perhaps we should consider that it is an attempt on the part of the Septuagint translators to reduce the Hebrew text figures (as to the origin of which we advanced a guess above) to a magnitude more in accord with the known realities of the situation by simply cutting the four hundred and thirty in half. If anything, the span of four generations might have been even somewhat less than two hundred and fifteen years. A modern reckoning, at any rate, would be more apt to allow something like thirty-three years for a generation, which would give a result of one hundred and thirty-two years. We may conclude, therefore, that our best attested fact is that the exodus took place in the fourth generation and that the period of residence in Egypt was somewhere between two hundred and fifteen and one hundred and thirty-two years in length.

When was this? In order to obtain at least an approximate indication of when the Israelites entered Egypt, we may use the figures just arrived at and count, on the one hand, forward from the time of Abraham, and, on the other hand, backward from the time of the exodus. In our study of the book of Genesis we concluded that the time of Abraham's entry into Canaan was probably around 1700 B.C.; counting forward two hundred and fifteen years to the descent of Jacob into Egypt would place the latter event soon after 1500 B.C. One of the items we noted as possibly confirmatory of the date just given for Abraham was the evidence of a great earthquake in the Near East around 1650 B.C. which could have overthrown Sodom and Gomorrah. When Abraham was a hundred years old Isaac was born (Genesis 21:5), and this was in the spring (Genesis 18:10) after the destruction of Sodom and Gomorrah, hence around 1650 B.C. Isaac was sixty years old when Jacob and Esau were born (Genesis 25:26), so that was around 1590 B.C. Jacob, in turn, was one hundred and thirty years old when he came to Egypt (Genesis 47:9), so this was around 1460 B.C. Some such date as this seems indicated by reckoning forward from the time of Abraham, and since his dates can, at best, be stated only in round numbers, we must allow at least some leeway in counting from this end. As to the time of the exodus, evidence will be given in the next chapter to show that this event probably took place under Pharaoh Ramses II and perhaps about 1270 B.C. Reckoning backward from one hundred and thirty-two to two hundred and fifteen years we would have dates from 1402 to 1485 B.C. for the entry of the Israelites into Egypt.

The inherent difficulties in such reckoning must be candidly admitted, and precise dates will at best be held only tentatively, yet it is with at least some assurance that we may place the coming of the Israelites to Egypt somewhere in the fifteenth century B.C., and with considerable assurance that we may place their exodus from that land in the earlier part of the thirteenth century. The situation in Egypt in those days may be recalled as follows. Somewhat prior to this time the Hyksos had been driven out. These invaders of obscure race from the East, as Manetho called them, had probably ruled Egypt from about 1730 to 1580 B.C. and were then expelled by Ahmose, who ranks as the founder of the Eighteenth Dynasty. Among the more famous rulers of this dynasty, with approximate dates B.C., were the queen Hatshepsut (1486-1468), and the kings, Thutmose III (1490-1436), Amenhotep III (1413-1377), Amenhotep IV (Akhenaton) (1380-1362), Tutankhamun (1362-1352), Eye (1352-1349), and Haremhab (1349-1319). Then came the Nineteenth Dynasty whose first rulers were Ramses I (1319-1318), Seti I (1318-1301), Ramses II (1301-1234), and Merneptah (1234-1222).[54]

The Hyksos are generally credited with the introduction of the horse and chariot into Egypt, and Ahmose, who expelled them, is described in an Egyptian text as riding abroad in his chariot, this being the first mention we have of the use of a chariot by an Egyptian king.[55] The facts that the king under whom Joseph served installed him in a chariot (Genesis 41:43) and that Joseph drove in his chariot to meet his father in Goshen (Genesis 46:29) are, therefore, quite in accord with the time somewhat after the expulsion of the Hyksos in which our chronology places him. The more exact dates of 1485 B.C. or 1402 B.C., whose very tentative character we have emphasized, would put Joseph's court service under Thutmose III or Amenhotep III, and some such time along in the middle of the Eighteenth Dynasty seems at least probable. In fact, a recent study of Genesis 37-50 from the point of view of the Egyptologist, finds that many customs, terms, proper names, and official titles in these chapters reflect so accurately the situation in the Eighteenth and Nineteenth Dynasties that we must assume a reliable tradition deriving from precisely these times; and as for the time of Joseph himself, a date under either Amenhotep III or Amenhotep IV is favored.[56]

How did the children of Israel fare in the land of Egypt? At first they evidently got along at least reasonably well. They were foreigners in the land, of course, but Asian immigrants such as they had often enough been received into Egypt as they came seeking sustenance and security. A willingness to welcome such a group as they were, seems to have prevailed in fact to the end of the Eighteenth Dynasty. The very last king of that dynasty, Haremhab, had a reputation for kindness to foreigners, and we have already noted the scene in his tomb in which Asiatics beg of him a home in Egypt "after the manner of your fathers' fathers since the beginning." The types and places of activity of the great kings of the Eighteenth Dynasty were also not such as to involve the children of Israel. Thutmose III campaigned much abroad; Amenhotep IV devoted himself to religious thought. The kings were builders, indeed, on a large scale, but Thutmose III and Amenhotep III built specially at Thebes where their mighty monuments are still to be seen, while Amenhotep IV erected a whole new capital at Akhetaton, and both of these places are in Upper Egypt far from the Delta.

So the comparative freedom and peace of the Israelites in this period, as reflected in the biblical record, fit well enough with what we can discern of the situation. Jacob himself lived on for seventeen years, then died at the age of one hundred and forty-seven (Genesis 47:28). Thereupon his sons all went freely up to Palestine, buried him in the cave of the field at Machpelah (Genesis 50:13), and all came freely back down again to their homes in Egypt. Joseph lived on to the age of one hundred and ten, died, and was embalmed after Egyptian custom and put in a coffin in Egypt (Genesis 50:26). After that, all his brothers and all that generation passed away (Exodus 1:6). But the descendants of Israel increased and grew numerous and strong (Exodus 1:7).

Then the situation changed, and in their later time in Egypt the children of Israel fared very badly. The change is marked in Exodus 1:8 by the statement that "there arose a new king over Egypt, who did not know Joseph." This can very well be taken as a reference to the beginning of a new dynasty and, if the children of Israel came into Egypt in the Eighteenth Dynasty, the new dynasty would be the Nineteenth. The most important kings of these two dynasties have already been listed, with approximate dates, above. In the Eighteenth Dynasty Thutmose III built a widespread empire, Amenhotep IV allowed it to disintegrate, and Haremhab rebuilt a strong government. Then the son of an army officer of Haremhab became the first king of the Nineteenth Dynasty and, with him, the famous name of Ramses was introduced into Egyptian history. Ramses I reigned only a couple of years, but he left the throne to his descendants, including Seti I, Ramses II, and Merneptah. These three kings all marched again in Asia and, with the renewed and even increased Asian orientation of Egypt, it is not surprising to find the northeastern Delta coming into increased importance as a center of governmental activity. Here, in fact, Ramses II built a new capital, of which more will be said in the next chapter, and did other works of construction as well. The geographical focus of this new activity was obviously such as to make probable the involvement of the Israelite people, given the location we have established as likely for them.

Also from the fifteenth century on to this very time and beyond, there is mention in Egyptian inscriptions of people who are called 'Apiru. This is a foreign term, equivalent to "Habiru" in Mesopotamia and Syria, probably meaning "ones who have crossed a border," i.e., "immigrants," and it is applied here to foreigners in Egypt. The word is obviously similar to "Hebrew," the name by which the children of Israel are frequently referred to in Egypt in the latter chapters of Genesis and the first chapters of Exodus. While the Israelites cannot have been the only "immigrants" in

Egypt, they were certainly in that sense of the word among the 'Apiru.

Furthermore, it is precisely Ramses II who speaks of the use of 'Apiru in his works of building: they "haul stones for the god Re, the Re of Ramses, the beloved of Amon, in the southern quarter of Memphis"; they "haul stones for the great fortress of the city of Ramses, the beloved of Amon."[57] Memphis was at the apex of the Delta, the "city of Ramses" was undoubtedly the new capital in the northeastern Delta, so here we have evidence of the labor of "immigrants" on temple and city construction in the time of Ramses II and in the general part of Egypt in which the Israelites lived. In fact, the reputation of Ramses II for the use of other than native Egyptians in his construction projects is still reflected in the Greek historians. Herodotus (II, 108) says that Sesostris (supposing this to refer to Ramses II) used foreigners on the canals he dug; and Diodorus reports concerning the building works of Ramses II: "The most difficult of all these works were executed by the captives whom he had brought from foreign regions, and he took care that the lapidary inscriptions should remind the reader that 'no Egyptian had a hand in them.' "[58]

The actual situation in Egypt and the implications of the biblical text are in very good agreement, therefore, if we understand the rise of a new king over Egypt in Exodus 1:8 to mean the change to the Nineteenth Dynasty, and if we refer to the time under the early kings of that dynasty the statement of Exodus 1:13: "They made the people of Israel serve with rigor, and made their lives bitter with hard service, in mortar and brick, and in all kinds of work in the field; in all their work they made them serve with rigor." It was for this reason that ever afterward when the Israelite people looked back to Egypt they called it "the house of bondage" (Exodus 13:3, etc.).

What was the result of their life in the house of bondage? If we make an outline of the book of Exodus the first six chapters may be considered as describing the bondage in Egypt. In the sixth chapter at the height of their oppression the plight of the children of Israel is described (in verse 9) in terms of "their broken spirit and their cruel bondage." In their enslavement they must indeed have been broken physically, psychologically, and spiritually. They were broken physically, for the lash of the taskmaster, the blazing sun, the terrible heat, the scanty provisions, and the impossible quotas took their toll, and undoubtedly many perished. They were broken psychologically, for a power which enslaves in that manner must try to enslave the mind as well as the body, and, if one endures slavery of body long enough, does not one also develop a slave mentality? They were broken spiritually. According to the King James Version of Exodus 6:9 they experienced an "anguish of spirit," and they surely were tormented in any belief they may have retained in a good God. The Hebrew is literally "shortness of spirit." They were about to run out of spirit. One does not know how much longer they could have been expected to hold out.

Was there any ground for expectation of anything better? There was at least a situation of challenge and response. The historian, Toynbee, and the sociologist, Sorokin, have both pointed out that peoples have often grown greater against hardship than in luxury (if they do not perish all together, we may add). Thus Josephus (in a passage where he uses the longer and less likely of his two figures for the duration of the captivity) describes the experience in Egypt as a sort of contest of the spirit: "For full four hundred years they endured these hardships: it was indeed a contest between them, the Egyptians striving to kill off the Israelites with drudgery, and these ever to show themselves superior to their tasks."[59]

People were there too. This is an obvious fact but it is not unimportant, for, where there are people, one never knows who may arise, or what someone may do.

And God was there. The statement of the immediately preceding paragraph is intended to prepare for the introduction in the next chapter of the person of Moses. He is the person who arises to do something in an otherwise intolerable and apparently hopeless situation, and the book of Exodus has much to tell about him. But even in all the stories in which the work of Moses is portrayed with such admiration, it should be remembered, as Gerhard von Rad insists in his book on *Moses,* that it is not Moses but God who is actually the central figure.[60] Most of all it is the words and deeds of God which the writers intend to set forth. God, according to the biblical narrative, was there, although it must scarcely have looked like it. He had made his covenant with Abraham and he had not forgotten his people. When God is still working at a matter, one never knows what may yet come to pass.

# 2  PHARAOH AND MOSES
## (Exodus 2-6)

As the oppression of the children of Israel in Egypt reached its climax, the opposing forces were represented by two great personalities: on the one hand, the embodiment of Egyptian power, Pharaoh; on the other hand, the protagonist of Israelite freedom, Moses. We look first at Pharaoh.

Who was Pharaoh? In the preceding chapter we judged it probable that the Israelites entered Egypt and were treated there with some favor in what is designated in Egyptian history as the Eighteenth Dynasty; and that they were increasingly oppressed under the earlier kings of the Nineteenth Dynasty. Seti I and Ramses II in particular were kings whose large building activities in the Delta would have made it likely that they would utilize the "immigrant" labor available there in the persons of the children of Israel. It was also indicated that reason would be given in the present chapter for centering attention specifically upon Ramses II as the probable king under whom the oppression reached its height and the exodus was actually made. It is to the considerations bearing upon this identification, and then to the characterization of the person so identified, that we are now turning.

The king in question was someone whom the Bible calls "Pharaoh" and who presumably actually carried that title. In all the first fifteen chapters of Exodus, which tell of the bondage (chapters 1-6), the plagues (chapters 7-12), and the escape (chapters 13-15), the king of Egypt is never once named by his personal name but always referred to simply by this title. The matter of the name and title of an Egyptian king is not uncomplicated. As to his name, the situation was much as it is with us to the extent that he had both a main or

family name (nomen), and a first name (prenomen); but it was
different in that the main name was bestowed at birth, the first
name only when he became king. The names of the king were
naturally regarded as very special, so to separate them from ordinary
words, when written, a line was drawn around them in an oval or
oblong, forming what is called a cartouche.

As to title, it was customary to employ a number of honorary
epithets. Five of these were specially prominent, and to understand
them we need chiefly only to remember that the king of Egypt was
thought of as a god, and that the land over which he ruled was
constituted by the union of two parts which had existed separately at
an earlier time, namely, Upper Egypt and Lower Egypt. The five
titles were: (1) "Horus," meaning that the king was the incarna-
tion of the sky god seen in the falcon; (2) "the Two Ladies," a
rather surprising title perhaps, which referred to the ruler as the
embodiment of the vulture goddess of Upper Egypt and the cobra
goddess of Lower Egypt; (3) "Horus of Gold," in allusion to the
brightness of his divinity; (4) "He of the Sedge and the Bee," em-
ploying the symbols of Upper and Lower Egypt; and (5) "Son of
Re," indicating that the king was descended from the sun god.
When this whole nomenclature was written out, the first four titles
were put down, then the first name (prenomen) in a cartouche, then
the fifth title, and finally the main name (nomen) in a cartouche. In
addition, the royal name was often followed by the interjection of a
wish for "life, prosperity, health!" Beyond that, other titles and
epithets might also be introduced almost without limit.

For an example, we may cite the titulary of Ramses II (with whom
we will be specially concerned later in this chapter) as it is given
on a stela which was found at Kuban, sixty miles above the First
Cataract. The subject of the inscription is only the excavation of a
well in the Wadi 'Alaqi to the east, but the king is introduced with a
full array of titles. In quoting this material we will number the titles
which correspond to the five given above, and italicize the prenomen
and nomen. In this way it may be seen that the titulary structure
explained above has been retained, but that additional titles have
been inserted within it and added to it in a carefully symmetrical
way.

(1) Horus: Mighty Bull, Beloved of Truth; (2) Favorite of the
Two Goddesses: Defender of Egypt, Binder of the Barbarians;
(3) Golden Horus: Rich in Years, Great of Victory; (4) King of
Upper and Lower Egypt: *User-maat-Re Setep-en-Re;* (5) Son of

Re: *Meri-Amon Ramses,* given life, forever and ever, beloved of Amon-Re, lord of Thebes, and presider over Karnak; shining upon the Horus-throne of the living, like his father, Re, every day; good god, lord of the Southland, Horus of Edfu, of brilliant plumage, beautiful hawk of electrum.[1]

In view of this extreme elaboration of entitlement, it is not surprising that a shorter way of referring to the king was also developed and increasingly used for convenience. In the Old Kingdom it was the custom to call the palace of the king the Great House even as we call the residence of the president of the United States the White House. Then, even as we may say that "the White House" says, they came to use "the Great House" as a respectful and brief expression for the king. In Egyptian this name was written as *per-o,* and it is this name which is transliterated in the Hebrew and Greek texts of the Old Testament and which comes to us in English as Pharaoh. According to the available evidence, the practice just described came into usage in the late Eighteenth Dynasty (e.g., in a letter to Amenhotep IV) and in the Nineteenth Dynasty. It was of course possible to use this title anachronistically, and it seems necessary to explain its usage in Genesis 12, in the earlier time of Abraham, in this way. For the time of Joseph, however, at least if he is to be put as late as Amenhotep IV (which was indicated as possible in the preceding chapter), and assuredly for the time of Moses, if he belongs indeed in the Nineteenth Dynasty, the designation of the king of Egypt as Pharaoh is eminently correct.

But can we identify any particular Pharaoh? I think we can because we can recognize the name of a Pharaoh in the name of a place where the Israelites labored at the worst of their oppression. The bitterness of the Egyptian servitude is epitomized in Exodus 1:11 in this statement: "Therefore they set taskmasters over them to afflict them with heavy burdens; and they built for Pharaoh store cities, Pithom and Raamses." Pithom was discussed in the preceding chapter, and we saw that this place name contains the name of a god, Tum or Atum, and not of a man. Raamses, however, is an only slightly variant form of the name of a man and a king. To recall the essentials of Egyptian history at this point again, after Amenhotep IV (with whom we can attest the title Pharaoh) the Eighteenth Dynasty deteriorated, but Egypt was rescued by a strong man of the army, the general and later the king, Haremhab. After himself he put on the throne, lacking a son of his own, the son of one of his officers. This man was Ramses I, first king of the

Nineteenth Dynasty, and his son and successor was Seti I, and in turn his son and successor was Ramses II. Now Ramses II did build a capital city in the Delta area and it was called by his own name. Of it we will tell more below.

Therefore, it seems probable that, although his predecessors doubtless played their parts in the development of events, the final and chief Pharaoh under whom the oppression reached its worst and from whom escape was made, was Ramses II, the king whose full name was, as we have seen, User-maat-Re Setep-en-Re Meri-Amon Ramses. This is further supported by the fact that the next Pharaoh, Merneptah, mentions in the fifth year of his reign that he laid waste to Israel up in Palestine; hence the Israelites must have gotten there by then.

If this is the correct answer as to who was Pharaoh, we may go on to ask, When did he live? In the preceding chapter, for ready reference and without raising questions of Egyptian chronology in detail, a list of the most important kings of the Eighteenth and Nineteenth Dynasties was given, with approximate dates as found in a standard history of ancient Egypt. Here, since we are particularly interested in Ramses II, we may note briefly that the most recent investigations of specialists in ancient Egyptian and Near Eastern chronology, indicate a slight revision in the date of this king. The standard listing given above put the accession of Ramses II around 1301 B.C. In the meantime, however, Richard A. Parker has shown that the mention in a Leiden papyrus of a certain date in the fifty-second year of Ramses II as being the new moon day (in Egypt this was probably the day when the last crescent of the waning moon was no longer to be seen in the eastern sky just before sunrise) would not be possible, astronomically, if the first year of his reign were 1301; it would be possible if his first year was either 1304 or 1290.[2] As between these two possible dates, M. B. Rowton then showed by comparisons with Mesopotamian chronology that it is necessary to choose the earlier, and he, accordingly, regards the year 1304 for the accession of Ramses II as an exact date.[3] It is well established that Ramses II occupied the throne for sixty-seven years; therefore, we may now date his reign 1304-1237 B.C.; and his mummy indicates that he was about ninety years of age when he died.[4]

What did Ramses II do? What he did abroad is of lesser interest in relation to our concerns but may be indicated briefly by saying that he fought on the frontiers to maintain Egyptian power. His most famous battle took place in the fifth year of his reign. The enemy were the Hittites, whose center was in Asia Minor. He marched four hundred miles north and met them at Kadesh on the Orontes River in Syria. The modern historian says that Ramses II walked into an ambush but—not without considerable bravery—cut his way out and saved himself and most of his army. He himself said—when he got safely back to Egypt and was far enough away from the scene to make his story hold—that he had won a great and glorious victory, and many of the carvings on his buildings (which we are about to mention) are occupied with depicting the event. In the twenty-first year of his reign, when both had grown more afraid of a common enemy, the Sea Peoples, than of each other, Ramses II and the Hittites signed a treaty of "good peace and brotherhood." To save face, each said that the other had suggested it. It provided for mutual nonaggression and mutual military assistance, and is considered the earliest such international treaty in the world. Later, the good relations between Egypt and the Hittites were further cemented when Ramses II married, as one of his many wives, a daughter of the Hittite king.[5]

What Ramses II did at home is of greater concern to us. Here one word above all suffices to describe his activity, and that is to say that he built. Of his buildings the outstanding characteristic has been indicated by the remark that they attempted to make an impression by overpowering size rather than by artistic quality.[6] Yet as one sees them—for many still stand or have been excavated in Egypt—there is an undeniable grandeur and majesty about them. Thebes in Upper Egypt was the ancient capital. The site is three hundred and fifty miles up the Nile from Cairo and is marked by the present town of Luxor (the name comes from el-Aksur, plural of the Arabic *kasr,* meaning "the castles"), whose main street is the ancient avenue. Near the riverbank is a temple nearly one thousand feet long. The massive pylon of the temple, which looms far above one, was built by Ramses II, and in front of it are colossal statues of himself. Farther downstream is the village of Karnak where there are three more temples of which the chief is "the greatest of all known temples," and here Ramses I, Seti I, and Ramses II built the enormous Hall of Columns which is "one of the wonders of the world."[7] Into it the entire cathedral of Notre Dame could be fitted with room to spare; on top of each of the seventy-foot columns which form its center aisle, one hundred men could stand; on the interior surfaces are six acres of painted relief sculpture.[8] Across the river on the western side Ramses II built his mortuary temple, known as the

Ramesseum. Here great reliefs portray the military exploits of the king, and here lies the fallen head of a colossal statue, estimated to have weighed a thousand tons.

On up the Nile, in what we call Nubia, were more monuments, intended to impress the tribes living beyond. Between the First and Second Cataracts, in the region which the new high dam at Aswan will begin to flood in 1963, are no less than six temples, the greatest at Abu Simbel. The Abu Simbel temple is cut out of the solid rock. Its inner chamber penetrates one hundred and eighty-five feet into the rock. In front, on the cliff overlooking the river, are four colossal seated statues of Ramses II. Seen in best perspective from the air, each is as tall as a six-story office building, and an ear is over three feet high. A recent visitor who saw it first from a boat rounding the bend in the river, and afterward in the evening from the sand at its foot, speaks of the awesome and unforgettable character of this monument.[9]

But it is in the Delta that, although the monuments are not now so well preserved, Ramses II seems to have been most interested (since he built there a whole new capital), and that we are certainly most interested (since the children of Israel resided in that region). The basic reason for the focusing here of Egyptian interest was presumably that relations with Asia were more important than ever, and this area was nearer to Asia. Also there may well have been an aversion to the very region where the hated Hyksos had been settled, which persisted during the Eighteenth Dynasty (note, for example, the indignation with which Hatshepsut refers in an inscription in her temple at Speos Artemidos in Middle Egypt to the former time when the Asians were in the Northland[10]), but which was no longer a factor in the Nineteenth Dynasty.

In this connection the situation with regard to the god Seth may be noted. Seth or Set is known from the earliest times. In the Pyramid Texts he is mentioned frequently and in close association with Horus and Osiris: Upper and Lower Egypt are respectively "the regions of Set" and "the regions of Horus," as the underworld is "the regions of Osiris."[11] In the celestial world the abode of Seth was a star in the constellation we know as the Great Bear and, from this location in the northern sky, the god was connected with cold, rain, and darkness. From a power of darkness in nature he became a symbol of evil in the moral realm and, in mythology, he became the murderer of his brother, Osiris. He was also identified with various Asian gods and, under the Hyksos, he became virtually the national god of the

Delta. It was recorded of the Hyksos king Apophis, for example, that "he would not serve any god who was in the land [except] Seth."[12]

Through his association with natural and moral darkness and particularly through his adoption by the Hyksos, it is understandable that Seth became much disliked among the native Egyptians, and this remained true throughout most of the Eighteenth Dynasty when Amon of Upper Egypt had the great pre-eminence. But at the end of the Eighteenth Dynasty and in the Nineteenth the cult of Seth was revived. Already under Haremhab there was a vizier who was named Sethi or Seti, which means "Seth's Man," and it was his father who became Pharaoh Ramses I and he himself who became Pharaoh Seti I.[13] Thus the name of the Delta god was carried into the royal nomenclature of the Nineteenth Dynasty. In a relief at Thebes Seti I stands between Horus and Seth while each pours a libation of "life" over his head; in another scene Ramses II receives the double crown of the South and the North from the same two gods.[14] If then, as all of this suggests, the royal family of the Nineteenth Dynasty was specially devoted to the worship of the god Seth who had become so closely connected with the Delta, there was all the more reason for a focus of interest in that region.

We have already noted that, according to Exodus 1:11, the specific cities in the construction of which Israelite labor was involved were Pithom and Raamses. In the Greek text of the same passage there is added: "On, which is Heliopolis." Pithom was dealt with in our previous chapter, where we identified the biblical land of Goshen with Wadi Tumilat and found Pithom, in probability, at Tell er-Retabeh at about the mid-point of that valley. On was a very ancient religious center of Lower Egypt, and its ruins are in the vicinity of the village of Matariyeh, a half-dozen miles northeast of Cairo. As also stated in the preceding chapter, this was the home of the god Atum, who was recognized as a form of the sun god. It was as a center of sun worship that the Greeks called On by the name of Heliopolis, the City of the Sun. It could be because the god Atum was worshiped both at Pithom and at On that the Septuagint extended the labors of the Israelites to include the latter place. But it could be that the Septuagint embodies an authentic local tradition in this regard, for Ramses II actually did building work at On as well as at Pithom and Raamses. This is shown by inscriptions of his on granite blocks of the ruined temple; in one carving he is offering a libation to Atum.[15] It remains, then, to discuss the city of Raamses.

There was an ancient Egyptian town called Hat-wa'ret, whose

name perhaps means "House of the River Arm."[16] It is mentioned
in the biography of Ahmose, a naval officer under the first kings of
the Eighteenth Dynasty, who fought there on the canal, as the text
records, in the siege and capture of the city.[17] This must be the same
town whose name is transcribed in the Greek text of Manetho as
Auaris or Avaris. According to Manetho, Avaris was rebuilt and forti-
fied by Salitis, the first king of the Hyksos, and was where the Hyksos
made their last stand in Egypt. After that, according to the same
source, Avaris remained, in the Eighteenth Dynasty, a "deserted
city."[18] This city, the capital of the Hyksos, must have been somewhere in the northeastern Delta where the invaders were centered.

That Ramses II built an important city which was known by his
own name is shown by his inscriptions. The first mention of it is in
a long inscription which he carved in the temple of his father, Seti
I, at Abydos. This tells how, in the first year of his reign, Ramses II
visited Thebes and erected a statue of his father there (as he also
did in Memphis), then went to Abydos where he undertook to complete the beautiful temple of Seti I which had been left unfinished.
When he sailed from Thebes down the Nile and to Abydos by a connecting canal there is a reference which apparently indicates that
he was also going on farther north to the Delta, and it is in this
passage that the name of his city occurs: "[He] began the way, to
make the voyage, while the royal barges illuminated the flood, turning downstream to the seat of might, 'Per-Ramses Meri-Amon Great-
of-Victory.' "[19] In this name of the city, Per-Ramses (also Pi-
Ra'messe, etc.) means "House of Ramses," and is followed by
epithets of the king, "Beloved-of-Amon" and "Great-of-Victory."

There is also mention of the city in a record of the treaty of
Ramses II with the Hittites which is carved on a wall of the temple
at Karnak. Here the arrival of the Hittite messengers who came to
negotiate the treaty is introduced by this statement: "On this day,
while his majesty was in the town of Per-Ramses Meri-Amon, doing
the pleasure of his father Amon-Re; Har-akhti; Atum, Lord of the
Two Lands, the Heliopolitan; Amon of Ramses Meri-Amon; Ptah of
Ramses Meri-Amon; and [Seth], the Great of Strength, the Son of
Nut, according as they give him an eternity of jubilees and an
infinity of years of peace, while all lands and all foreign countries
are prostrate under his soles forever—there came the Royal Envoy
and Deputy. . . ."[20] Here, not only is Ramses II described as present
in his capital city when the Hittite delegates come, but the gods
Amon and Ptah are mentioned in the forms in which they are wor-

shiped here, and thus the name of the city occurs three times. Again on a stela in the first hall of the great temple of Ramses II at Abu Simbel, the god Ptah makes address to the king and refers to the construction of the city: "Thou hast made an august residence, to make strong the boundary of the Two Lands [named]: 'Per-Ramses Meri-Amon Given-Life,' that it may flourish on earth like the four pillars of heaven."[21] From the facts found in these inscriptions that Ramses II was to sail north to reach the city, that the Hittite messengers coming in from Asia met him there, and that it was a stronghold of the boundary of Egypt, we would naturally place the city in the northeastern Delta.

There is also an inscription of Ramses II on a ruined wall of a temple of Ptah at Memphis which in its extant portion lists and represents a series of fourteen districts of Lower Egypt. Each district is represented by a human figure with a name above it, who offers the name of Ramses II between two vases, with a text which states that the king presents that place as an offering to the god Ptah. In this list the third name is Sekhet-Za ($\acute{S}ht\ D'$) or the "Field-of-Za'" and the fourth is Avaris.[22] In addition there are two statues (possibly of the fourth century B.C.) in the Cairo Museum which carry such similar titles that for geographical purposes they may justifiably be used together, and on one there is mention of Per-Ramses and on the other of the Sekhet-Za'anet ($\acute{S}ht\ D'nt$) or the "Field-of-Za'anet."[23]

Since "Field-of-Za'" and "Field-of-Za'anet" are probably equivalent terms, and since they are connected in the one case with Avaris, and in the other with Per-Ramses, the identity of Avaris and Per-Ramses is also suggested. If this is correct, Avaris and Per-Ramses were the successive names of a city which was located in or near the Field of Za'anet. In agreement with these facts, the Sekhet-Za'anet or "Field-of-Za'anet" is clearly mentioned in Psalm 78:12, 43, where the region is called in Hebrew transcription the $\acute{s}dh\ \d{s}'n$ or "the fields of Zoan" and in the Septuagint version (Psalm 77:12, 43) "the plain of Tanis," and where it is stated that this was the place where the marvels of the Lord were wrought for the fathers of the people of Israel.

From the name of this adjacent region the name Za'anet evidently became attached also to the city itself. In a hieratic papyrus of the Twenty-first Dynasty the journey of a certain Wen-Amon from Karnak to Byblos is narrated, and in this he tells of reaching $D'nt$ where Ne-su-Ba-neb-Ded was.[24] The latter is identified with Smendes whom Manetho names as the first of the seven kings of the

Twenty-first Dynasty who ruled at Tanis.[25] Therefore *D'nt* or
Za'anet must be the Egyptian name of the Delta capital known in
Greek as Tanis. An Assyrian transcription of the name of the city as
Ṣa'anu is found in the records of Ashurbanipal;[26] and the city is
mentioned as Zoan in the Hebrew and Tanis in the Greek text of a
number of passages in the Old Testament (Numbers 13:22, where
Hebron is said to have been built seven years before Zoan; Isaiah
19:11, 13; 30:4; Ezekiel 30:14).

If, then, the foregoing identifications are correct, the ancient
Egyptian Hat-wa'ret and the Hyksos Avaris, the Nineteenth Dynasty
Per-Ramses, and the later *D'nt* or Za'anet, Sa'anu, Zoan, and Tanis,
are the names in successive periods of one and the same place. To
complete the series, there is a present-day village in the northeastern
Delta, on the Muwis Canal, which probably represents the ancient
Tanitic (or, Saïtic) arm of the Nile,[27] the name of which is San el-
Hagar. Here the Arabic *ṣan* is clearly the equivalent of the Hebrew
*ṣn* or Zoan, while the qualifying remainder of the name (el-
Hagar, meaning "of stone"[28]) may refer to the ancient ruins of the
adjacent tell. Here, as the excavations which we will shortly report
have indicated, is the probable location of the ancient Avaris—Per-
Ramses—Tanis.

It may be noted that when Manetho introduces Avaris he describes it as "in the Saïte nome" and "on the east of the Bubastite
branch of the Nile."[29] If "Saïte" refers to the Egyptian city of Saïs,
this would point to the western Delta where this well-known city
was located on the Canopic branch of the Nile, and was the capital
of the Lower Egyptian Nome V, the nome of the goddess Neith.[30]
But in listing the mouths of the Nile in the eastern Delta, Strabo
(XVII, i, 20 [802]) writes: "Then follows the Tanitic mouth, which
some call the Saïtic, and the Tanite nome, and in it a large city
Tanis." This shows that Saïte and Tanite could simply be variant
forms of one name, with Greek Sigma and Tau alternate transcrip-
tions of the same Egyptian character, and thus the Saïte nome and
the Tanite nome were one and the same. As for the "Bubastite
branch" of the Nile, this is often assumed to be the Pelusiac which
flowed past Bubastis and went on, at a considerable distance to the
east of Tanis, to enter the Mediterranean near Pelusium (as we saw
in the preceding chapter). But we have now seen that the ancient
Tanite branch is probably represented by the present Muwis Canal,
and this passes close by the west side of Tell Basta (Bubastis) and
then by the west side of the tell of San. Therefore, it was possible

to go by boat from Tanis to Bubastis on the Tanitic branch, and this could have been called the Bubastite branch. In this case, if Avaris was at San it was in fact on the east of the Bubastite branch.[31]

As to the nome in which Tanis was located, called by Manetho the Saïte or Tanite nome, this is probably to be identified with Nome XIV of the ancient Egyptian administrative districts. Nome XIV was also known as Khant-yeb, or as "the eastern Khant nome," as it is called already on the Palermo Stone;[32] its chief god was Horus in a warlike form, known as Horus of Mesen and called "the Watcher of the Gates of Egypt";[33] and its capital was a place whose Egyptian name has been transcribed as Tjaru or, better, as Thel, which appears in itineraries of the Roman period as Sile, and which has been identified with Tell Abu Seifeh, one and a half miles east of Kantarah on the present Suez Canal.[34]

That Tanis belonged to this nome is suggested by various references. In a number of texts the Field of Za' or Field of Za'anet (which, as we have seen, was adjacent to and the source of the name of the city of Tanis) is spoken of as the *peḥu* (meaning something like "hinterland") of Nome XIV: for example, in a long geographical text of Edfu, it is said of the nome god, Horus of Mesen, that "he inundates the Phoenix-land at its season of the year, he pours its fresh water into the *peḥu* of Field-of-Za'."[35] In the Edfu text and elsewhere there is also mention of Shi-Hor or the "Waters-of-Horus" as being in Nome XIV and as being the water upon which floats the sacred bark, "Beautiful-is-Mesen."[36] Then in the description of the residence city of Ramses II in Papyrus Anastasi III, it is said in closest connection with Per-Ramses: "The Shi-hor has salt, and the Her canal has natron. . . . The reed-thicket comes to it with papyrus; the Shi-Hor with rushes."[37] The Shi-Hor, therefore, was perhaps the Tanite branch of the Nile with its salt flats and papyrus marshes or perhaps, more extensively, whatever corresponded in ancient times to Lake Menzaleh.[38]

Incidentally, the name Shi-Hor is taken over directly into Hebrew and occurs a number of times in the Old Testament, for example in Joshua 13:3 where it has to do with the border of Egypt and is spoken of as "the Shihor, which is before Egypt." Also the term in Papyrus Anastasi III which is translated "reed-thicket" or "reed-swamps" is the same word (Egyptian *t w f*; Hebrew *suph*) which is found in the Old Testament in the name of the Yam Suph or Reed Sea (see below in Chapter 6).

In objection to placing Tanis in Nome XIV it might be said that

San (which we think to be the site of ancient Tanis) is too far distant (nearly thirty miles west and north) from Tell Abu Seifeh (which was doubtless the site of Thel, the capital of the nome); but even as Thel was on the extreme eastern border so Tanis may simply have been near the limits of the nome at the other side. In objection to identifying Avaris with Tanis it has been said that the inscription on the temple of Ptah at Memphis (cited above, page 31) lists Tanis and Avaris as separate localities;[39] but as has been correctly stated already, the names are actually "Field-of-Za' " and Avaris, and it seems eminently correct and in accord with the hypothesis which we have followed that there is mentioned here first the region, the "Field-of-Za' " (or "Field-of-Za'anet," as it is called in other sources), and then the city, Avaris, which was located in or near the region.[40]

Similarly, there could be raised in objection to the identification of Per-Ramses with Tanis the fact that in Judith 1:9-10 Raamses and Tanis are mentioned separately; but here again it is at least not certain but that the first name might mean a region (cf. "the land of Rameses" in Genesis 47:11) and the second the city. So in spite of some possible difficulties the evidence thus far considered makes it probable that the residence city which Ramses II built in the Delta and to which he gave his name, Per-Ramses, was formerly the Hyksos capital of Avaris and the Egyptian town Hat-wa'ret, and afterward the city known from the adjacent region as Za'anet or Zoan (in Hebrew) or Tanis (in Greek). Since the present Delta village of San preserves this last name in an Arabic form, and since beside the village there is a very large tell, the archeological exploration of this ancient mound was obviously indicated.

San el-Hagar is seventy-five miles northeast of Cairo, thirty miles northeast of Zagazig, and thirty miles north and a little west of Tell er-Retabeh (which we think represents Ramses' other city of Pithom). Like the village, the adjacent mound, Tell-es-San, lies at a curve of the Muwis Canal, and we have already seen that this probably represents the ancient Tanitic branch of the Nile. The first excavation was conducted here by Auguste Mariette in 1861; in 1869 Emmanuel de Rougé reported on inscriptions he had copied at the place;[41] and in 1884 W. M. Flinders Petrie made a further examination of the ruins.[42] Four sphinxes, or lions with kings' heads, were found which are now in the Cairo Museum and are believed to date from the Twelfth Dynasty and probably from the reign of Amenemhet III.[43] Two colossal statues of black granite, also in the Cairo Museum, bear the name of Mermeshau, probably of the Thirteenth Dynasty, but were successively used by, and inscribed with the names of, Apophis, the last of the Hyksos kings, and of Ramses II.[44] Another black granite statue carries the titles of Senusert I of the Twelfth Dynasty but was reused by Merneptah, who writes: "Merneptah, beloved of Set, lord of Hat-wa'ret. . . ."[45] Other inscriptions recorded by de Rougé mention "Seth, Lord of Hat-wa'ret."[46] Most numerous were the inscriptions of Ramses II who had erected, as the discovered remains showed, at least four stelae commemorating his ability in war,[47] and fourteen obelisks.[48]

One other stela of considerable importance was unearthed by Mariette, copied and published, then reburied, and only dug up again by Pierre Montet. In a relief at the top of it Ramses II and an official named Seti stand before the god Seth who is shown in Asian garb and designated as "Seth of Ramses," thus being located in the city of Per-Ramses. In the inscription below, which is not too easy to interpret, Seti tells how he was commissioned to erect a great granite stela here in honor of Seti I, the father of Ramses II. Then he continues with a prayer to the god Seth, in the course of which he calls himself the "commandant of the fortress of Tjaru (i.e., Thel or Sile)" and also mentions a celebration of the four hundredth year of the rule of the god Seth as king. The celebration may have been conducted by the vizier Seti (who became Pharaoh Seti I) under Haremhab, say around 1330 B.C.; four hundred years before would be about 1730 B.C., which would be the time of the arrival of the Hyksos and could be the time when they founded their capital here at Avaris where Seth was so strongly worshiped. Upon the fact of this four-hundred-year sway of Seth, Ramses II apparently now based the claim of this place to be the capital.[49] Thus, even in the early explorations at Tell es-San, the findings seemed in accord with the hypothesis that this was the site of the Delta city with which we are concerned. The name Hat-wa'ret was found, the special worship of Seth was attested, and records of the Hyksos king, Apophis, and of Ramses II were found.

Following upon this earlier work, in 1929 extensive excavation of Tell es-San was undertaken by the University of Strasbourg under the direction of Pierre Montet and continued until 1951.[50] In these excavations Montet found what he considered to be numerous traces of Asian influence. A wide enclosure wall of unbaked brick surrounded the principal temple, and along its inner side were two burials which, like the similar one at Tell er-Retabeh (mentioned in our preceding chapter), may have been foundation sacrifices. Since such a practice was Asian and not Egyptian as far as we know, this was judged by Montet to be proof of Semitic influence, and Raymond Weill[51] has expressed agreement at least this far, while Alan H. Gardiner[52] seems to regard the evidence as definitely indicating that the great fortifications were built by the Hyksos. Montet also states that the signatures of the Hyksos kings are more numerous at Tell es-San than in any other city.[53] All of this accords well with the identification of San with Avaris.

As for the identification with Per-Ramses, it appears to be confirmed even more strongly by the work of Montet. Like the earlier excavators, he too found many ruins bearing the name of Ramses II. As he traced it, the royal domain of Ramses II was thirty-two acres in extent, and within it stood the great temple which was one thousand three hundred feet in length. Here Ramses II built a great colonnade with columns like the trunks of palm trees and erected obelisks, as already mentioned, the broken pieces of which indicate they were probably one hundred and fifty feet high. Concerning Tanis it has, in fact, been said that "no Egyptian city but Thebes itself can boast a greater number of stelae, statues, sphinxes, and architectural remains bearing the cartouches of Ramesses II and his successors."[54]

There was also one statue which is of particular interest since its owner, a certain Pikha'as, son of Pakem, identifies himself as "governor of the nome of Khant-yeb, governor of Tanis, doing the works at Sile."[55] As in the Stela of the Year Four Hundred, dealt with above, where a commandant of the fortress at Sile came on an official mission to Tanis, so here, where an official of Tanis exercises activity at Sile, the interrelations of the two places are indicated and the location of Tanis in the nome of which Sile was the capital seems to be confirmed.

The excavations of Montet showed also that Tanis remained a capital of great importance long after the time of Ramses II. In the Twenty-first Dynasty, Psusennes I was buried here, and his beautiful tomb was found still intact; in the Twenty-second Dynasty the last Sheshonk, or one of the last kings of this name, built a vast temple of which numerous building blocks were recovered; and in the Twenty-fifth Dynasty a stela of Taharqo shows the continued eminence of the city.[56] Likewise, the biblical references attest the importance of Tanis in the times of Isaiah (19:11, 13) and Ezekiel (30:14).

There are also ruins twelve miles south of San el-Hagar at the village of Qantir. Here, excavations by the Egyptian archeologist, Mahmud Hamza, found the remains of a large palace of Ramses II, and of the factory which made the colored glazed tiles and glazed statues with which this palace was adorned. In addition, five inscribed fragments of pottery jars were uncovered which actually bore the name, Per-Ramses.[57] Since these inscriptions indicated the provenance of the wine which the jars contained, it seems to be suggested that Per-Ramses was at least somewhere in the vicinity. Some scholars, in fact, would wish to identify Per-Ramses with these ruins rather than with those at Tell es-San.[58] It may be noted, however, that the distance of twelve miles between Qantir and San el-Hagar is not greater than the distance between the boundary stones which still mark out the area of the capital which Amenhotep IV built at Akhetaton (Tell el-Amarna); and since, as far as the excavations have gone, the chief building at Qantir was a palace, and at San a temple, it could be that the city of Ramses actually included both of these sites, Qantir being primarily the residential place and San the religious center.[59] Such, then, was the possible extent under Ramses II of his great Delta capital, the House-of-Ramses Beloved-of-Amon Great-of-Victory.

The famous city was praised in poetical compositions which are preserved on papyri of the end of the thirteenth century.[60] Papyrus Anastasi II uses Ramses' epithet "Great of Victory" as a name by itself for the city; locates it broadly as between Djahi, which means the Phoenician coast including Palestine, and Egypt; describes it as full of provisions in a way that reminds one of the biblical description of it as a store city; and engages in a doubtless pardonable exaggeration of its vast extent:

His majesty—life, prosperity, health!—has built himself a citadel, the name of which is "Great of Victory." It is between Djahi and Egypt, and is full of food and provisions. . . . The sun rises in its horizon, and sets within it. All men have left their towns and are settled in its territory.

In Papyrus Anastasi III a scribe tells of reaching Per-Ramses, as he names the city, and reports that the district is of unparalleled beauty. He writes in glowing terms of the abundantly productive fields, the lakes abounding with fish and birds, the papyrus thickets of the Shi-Hor (the water spoken of above in connection with our earlier quotation from this same source), and the ships which constantly go out and come back to mooring, to ensure unfailing supplies. Then he portrays the fortunate inhabitants who feel no lack of anything, and who rejoice when their ruler comes into the city, and he concludes with an apostrophe to the king himself, using both his names User-maat-Re Setep-en-Re and Ramses Meri-Amon:

> One rejoices to dwell within it, and there is none who says: "Would that!" to it. The small in it are like the great. . . . The young men of "Great of Victory" are dressed up every day, with sweet oil upon their heads and newly dressed hair. They stand beside their doors, their hands bowed down with flowers . . . on the day when User-maat-Re Setep-en-Re . . . enters in. . . .
> So dwell content of heart and free, without stirring from it, O User-maat-Re Setep-en-Re . . . Ramses Meri-Amon . . . thou god!

Here, no doubt, at least after the conclusion of peace with the Hittites, in his splendid city Ramses II did dwell, without often departing from it, in the enjoyment of contentment and freedom.

What was Pharaoh Ramses II like? The modern historian remembers his sixty-seven years of reign; his more than one hundred sons, twelve of whom died before him and one of whom, Merneptah, succeeded him; his works of conquest and construction—and writes: "In his length of rule, in the vast progeny which carried his divine seed, and in the massive bulk of monuments bearing his name, he left a tremendous shadow across Egyptian history, so that pharaohs named themselves after him for more than a century, and he passed into legend as the great conquering and imperial pharaoh."[61]

Yet any realistic assessment made in terms of human values must emphasize that it was indeed a shadow which he cast over Egypt. In his book on *Moses*, André Neher reconstructs the social situation in the empire ruled by Ramses II as that of an almost totalitarian state in which the vast masses were forced into classes, the lowest of which were distinguished only by gradations of misery. The Egyptian proletariat is represented by those who say, in the papyrus of Turin, "we are putrefying with hunger"; yet theoretically, at least, they still had some value as human beings, and of the proletarian it was said, "He still has a heart." But of the slaves it was said, "They have no hearts"—the heart signifying the personality itself. Neher writes:

> In Egypt the proletariat is numerous. However, in their drawings there are spaces round the peasants and workmen who, in spite of their numbers, seem to retain a minimum of individuality. On the

other hand the scenes depicting slavery and forced labour are brutal in their massiveness. Human beings are so closely packed and piled upon each other that they appear as a single whole yoked as such to its work, without any individuality at all.

These human masses are the victims of the totalitarian empire of the Rameses and their passionate and fanatical cult of power. The State and its prestige demand the systematic construction of colossal depots, fortresses, palaces, temples, cities and tombs. The slaves provide the gratuitous and inexhaustible pool of labour for this immense task.[62]

Ramses II was the kind of man who could be at the top of a system of this kind. He may have dwelt in his great city "content of heart and free," but among the slaves who populated his labor camps there was only discontent and servitude of the bitterest kind. Among those slave people were the children of Israel, but from their midst came a man who was more than a match for Pharaoh.

As we turn now from Pharaoh, the embodiment of Egyptian power, to Moses, the protagonist of Israelite freedom, we shall ask about Moses the same sort of questions we asked about the Egyptian king. Who was Moses? Here we must sharpen this question to mean, Was he a real person? This has been denied. In 1906 Eduard Meyer declared that the question as to whether the biblical figure of Moses had back of it a historical personality of this name, was a question which lay entirely beyond the limits of historical knowledge. As far as he was concerned, Moses was not a historical personality. "Except for those who accept tradition bag and baggage as historical truth," he wrote, "no one of those who treat him as a historical figure has ever yet been able to fill him with any kind of content, to portray him in any concrete individuality, or to set forth anything which he could have created or which could have been his historical work."[63] In 1960 Martin Noth found the historical problem of the personality of Moses extraordinarily difficult to solve, and came to a conclusion which was also chiefly negative: "Historically, it is . . . hardly justifiable to describe him as the organizer and law-giver of Israel."[64]

The question as to the historical character of Moses is, of course, closely bound up with the question as to the sort of records which we have concerning him. For Ramses II the record of monuments and inscriptions still bearing his name is available. For Moses, although some have claimed it, it does not seem that his name has ever been found in any Egyptian source. D. I. Heath and F. J. Lauth thought they found his name in Egyptian papyri, and H. Grimme believed he discovered it in the Sinaitic inscriptions, but the readings are at best uncertain. Henry S. Noerdlinger thinks the picture of Moses could have been in a relief of the Karnak temple, but whatever was there once, was carved out long ago and another picture substituted, that of Ramses II himself.[65]

The basic records, therefore, are only those which are found in the Old Testament. Here we have the first five books which are often called the five books of Moses, and the traditional view was that Moses wrote them all. It was, of course, to be noticed that the fifth book concludes with an account of the death of Moses, which he could hardly have written himself; and it appears also as if there are two or more accounts of many things, which seem unlikely if one author wrote the whole. So Jean Astruc, who died in 1766, and Julius Wellhausen, who worked around 1875, and many others set forth the theory that the Pentateuch (as we may call these five books) was compiled from a number of different sources of different date. In a widely held form of this theory, these sources were the "J" document of around 850 B.C., the "E" document of around 750 B.C., the "D" document of about 621 B.C., and the "P" document of around 500 B.C. Since these dates are from four to seven centuries after the presumable time of Moses, it is possible to suppose, as Eduard Meyer did on this very basis, that they no longer contain anything of historical importance concerning Moses as a historical personality. Likewise Martin Noth believes that the Pentateuch was compiled step by step from a series of originally independent themes, and thinks that the regular appearance of Moses in most of these themes can be accounted for only as due to a process of later assimilation.

While there are certainly evidences of compilation in the Pentateuch, and while the materials therein must surely have been handed down over a period of time, the most important consideration in relation to our question about Moses would seem to be, not when all the materials were finally put together in the form in which we have them (of which process the documentary theory may give us some idea), but whether the transmitted materials actually fit the time they purport to tell about. When tested against the background from which they are supposed to come, are they congruent therewith? This is the same question which we asked about the traditions concerning Abraham in our study of the book of Genesis, and to which we there gave an affirmative answer. Concerning the Pentateuch as a whole, W. F. Albright has expressed the judgment:

The contents of our Pentateuch are, in general, very much older than the date at which they were finally edited; new discoveries continue to confirm the historical accuracy or the literary antiquity of detail after detail in it. Even when it is necessary to assume later additions to the original nucleus of Mosaic tradition, these additions reflect the normal growth of ancient institutions and practices, or the effort made by later scribes to save as much as possible of extant traditions about Moses. It is, accordingly, sheer hypercriticism to deny the substantially Mosaic character of the Pentateuchal tradition.[66]

So at the present point where we have to do with the life and work of Moses in the land of Egypt, our fundamental question is whether the records about him are congruent with the Egyptian background he is supposed to have lived in. To this question our answer is that the account of Moses seems as unmistakably relevant to Egypt as that of Abraham was related to Mesopotamia. Part of the documentation for this answer has already been given in our first chapter on "The House of Bondage" and in the preceding part of the present chapter. There we have seen that the presence of Asians and the use of foreigners for forced labor were normal features in Egypt at this time, and we have found that there are abundant and unmistakably related Egyptian materials to work with in the attempt to identify areas and sites named in the biblical account.

More particularly we may now note the character of some of the names in the story of Moses. His own name is in fact almost certainly an Egyptian name. If we look, for example, at a cartouche with the name of the well-known king, Thutmose III, we see a little picture of the ibis, the bird which represents the god Thoth, followed by a syllabic sign and an alphabetic sign. The syllabic sign, which is a verbal form, may be represented in our letters as *mś* and the alphabetic sign, which is added to indicate the pronunciation, as *ś*; when the vowels are supplied the word was probably *maśe* or *mośe*. The verb *mś* means "to bear, to give birth, to create," and the form used here is known as the old perfective; accordingly, the entire name may be translated to mean "[the god] Thoth has created" (Steindorff), or "Thoth is born" (Gardiner), the latter perhaps referring to the birthday of the god. Similarly, the name Ramses or Ramesses (*Rꜥ-ms-sw*) contains the same verbal stem but in the form of an active participle and means, referring to the sun god, "Re is he who has borne him."[67]

While in such compound forms as these -*mose* appears as only a part of the whole name, it could also stand alone as a name in and of itself. In such cases it is usually supposed that it is an abbreviation of what was originally a longer name, but whether or not that is true, it is certainly found independently in Egyptian sources. Thus in an inscription of the fourteenth year of Ramses II we read of "the priest Pa-ser, son of Mose"; and in Papyrus Anastasi I of the late Nineteenth Dynasty (end of the thirteenth century) we hear of the "son of the steward Mose."[68]

Therefore, it seems almost certain that the biblical Moses bears this same ancient Egyptian name. It is true that the Egyptian Mose is then transcribed in Hebrew as Mosheh (the *ś* being reproduced by *shin*), while Ramses or Ramesses is transcribed as Raamses (the *ś* being reproduced by *samekh*), but there are other examples of variation in the reproduction of the sibilant, so this does not seem a serious objection to the derivation of the Hebrew name from the Egyptian.[69] As for the Greek, the name is spelled both Moyses and Moses in the manuscripts of the Septuagint; and even so we have it as Moses in English.

Moses was a member of the tribe of Levi (Exodus 2:1 ff., etc.), and at least several other members of this same tribe have Egyptian names. In an epithet of Ramses II, we have seen that he was called Meri-Amon, meaning "beloved of the god Amon," and *Mry* as the abbreviation of a name of that type or as standing by itself and meaning simply "the beloved" was a common Egyptian personal name. The name of Merari, a son of Levi (Exodus 6:16) was evidently essentially the same as this. The wife of Eleazar, Aaron's son, was a daughter of Putiel. In Hebrew the first part of the name Putiel is spelled exactly the same as the first part of the Egyptian name Potiphera (Genesis 41:45); the El at the end, a name of God acceptable in Israel, may have replaced the name of some pagan deity in a fully Egyptian form of the name. The son of Eleazar and the daughter of Putiel was Phinehas. This is recognized as derived from *p'nhsy*, "the Nubian." Other names that were traditional among the Levites and that are judged "unquestionably Egyptian" are Assir, Pashhur, and Hophni.[70]

As for Semitic rather than Egyptian names, one of the Hebrew midwives in Exodus 1:15 was called Shiphrah, and virtually the same name has now been found in a list of "female Asian" slaves in Egypt in a papyrus of the Brooklyn Museum from the Thirteenth Dynasty (around 1740 B.C.).[71]

When the biblical materials are found to fit into the background of ancient Egypt in points of such detail as those we have just noted, the presumption is heightened that they do, in fact, transmit information of dependable character concerning the times and persons they purport to tell about. Moses, therefore, we may believe, was a real person about whom we can hope to know something. Toward such a conclusion, both Christian and Jewish scholars have recently pointed. In *A History of Israel*, published in 1959, John Bright, Professor of Old Testament in Union Theological Seminary, Richmond, Virginia, writes concerning the events of the exodus:

Over all these events there towers the figure of Moses. Though we know nothing of his career save what the Bible tells us, the details of which we have no means of testing, there can be no doubt that he was, as the Bible portrays him, the great founder of Israel's faith. Attempts to reduce him are subjective in the extreme. The events of exodus and Sinai require a great personality behind them. And a faith as unique as Israel's demands a founder as surely as does Christianity—or Islam, for that matter. To deny that role to Moses would force us to posit another person of the same name![72]

In *The Religion of Israel*, published in 1960, Yehezkel Kaufmann, Professor of Bible in the Hebrew University, Jerusalem, writes: "The historicity of Moses is vouched for by trustworthy historical facts."[73] That is the conclusion to which we have come.

When did Moses live? According to the theory we have presented, Moses must have been a contemporary of Ramses II and must, therefore, have lived around 1300 B.C. in round numbers. To be more precise and detailed is not altogether easy. Acts 7:23 states that Moses was forty years of age when he visited his own people and saw their oppression; Exodus 7:7 states that his age was eighty years when he returned from Midian and confronted Pharaoh; Deuteronomy 34:7 says that he was one hundred and twenty years of age when he died. That divides the life of Moses into three forty-year periods, which makes a convenient way to remember the outline of his life. The figure forty is used so frequently, however, in the Bible and in rabbinic literature too, that one feels justified in taking it as a round number which just means many years.[74]

The historical framework into which our theory supposes that the life of Moses must be fitted is that of the Nineteenth Dynasty in Egyptian history. In the Eighteenth Dynasty, we believe, the children of Israel entered Egypt and were treated well. The new king of Exodus 1:8, "who did not know Joseph," we understand to be the first king of a new dynasty, namely, the Nineteenth, in which a

different attitude prevailed toward the foreigners. Oppression began, and reached its climax under Ramses II, resulting in the exodus.
The sixty-seven-year reign of Ramses II is now dated, as we have
seen, 1304-1237 B.C. It was probably at least eighteen years before
that that Ramses I ascended the throne as the first king of the new
dynasty; it was in the fifth year of Ramses II's successor, Merneptah,
that Israel is mentioned as present in Palestine. From the beginning
of the dynasty when, by our theory, the oppression began, to the
time when the Israelites had reached Palestine, was, therefore,
ninety years. This is, at least approximately, the duration of the
reigns of Ramses I, Seti I, Ramses II, and of Merneptah to the fifth
year of his rule. Since, according to the biblical narrative, Moses
was born under the oppression and died on the eve of the entry into
Palestine, his life must fit into this span of ninety years. If we make
the maximum allowance and allot to Moses a life of ninety years,
we shall have reduced the biblical figure of one hundred and twenty
years by one-quarter and we shall have attributed to Moses a
longevity exactly equal to that already noted as probable for Ramses
II.

We are putting the birth of Moses, therefore, at the very beginning
of the Nineteenth Dynasty, under Ramses I. Of the family of this
king we do not know enough to identify further the daughter of
Pharaoh who found the small Moses in the basket among the reeds
(Exodus 2:5). In I Chronicles 4:18 there is mention of "Bithiah the
daughter of Pharaoh," who was married to Mered of the tribe of
Judah, and the Midrash Rabbah commenting on Exodus 2:10 con-
siders that this is the name of the princess who found Moses.[75]

According to Exodus 2:11, it was "when Moses had grown up"
that he visited his own people and saw their oppression. Acts 7:23
makes him forty years of age when this transpired, but the Midrash
Rabbah on Exodus 2:11 gives as the prevailing rabbinic opinion
that "Moses was twenty years old at the time," while "some say
forty."[76] One rabbi argued that he was only twelve. He translated the
question in Exodus 2:14 as "Who made you for a man?"; explained
it to mean "Who made you for a man, since you are only a minor?"
and concluded that Moses was still less than 13, the age of man-
hood.[77] Among these figures, that of twenty years of age may seem
to accord best with the impulsive and violent action which Moses
took at the time. In fact, according to our reconstruction, we should
place his flight from Egypt under Seti I, and perhaps about a year
before the accession of Ramses II in 1304 B.C., which would make

Moses about seventeen years of age. This would allow him to dwell in the land of Midian, where he married and had a son, for about a year before "the king of Egypt [namely, Seti I] died" (Exodus 2:23), and the next king (namely, Ramses II) came to the throne and so accentuated the oppression that at last the people were brought to the point of utter desperation.

Similarly, it would seem permissible to reduce, at least somewhat, the traditional periods of forty years each for the sojourn of Moses in Midian and for the wandering in the wilderness. Periods up to thirty or thirty-five years in each case would still be available within the framework we have suggested, which would mean that Moses could have returned to Egypt, confronted Pharaoh, and accomplished the exodus at some time up to around 1270 B.C., with arrival in Palestine coming by 1240 or 1235 B.C.

What did Moses do? He came into the world as an Israelite. One of the twelve sons of Jacob (or Israel) was Levi (Exodus 1:2), and the generations run on: Levi, Kohath, Amram (Exodus 6). Amram married his father's sister, Jochebed, and their sons were Aaron and Moses (Exodus 6:20). Moses grew up as an Egyptian. Pharaoh's daughter took him to raise (Exodus 2:10). He discovered his neighbor. One day when he was grown up he went out to his people and saw their burdens (Exodus 2:11). He discovered his God. Out in the wilderness, at Horeb, God called him and commissioned him (Exodus 3). Thereafter he entered into the struggle of human history on behalf of his people and his God. Of all of that we will have more to say in the following chapters.

What was Moses like? He was a man of very human traits whose anger, for example, is not glossed over in the record (Exodus 2:12; 11:8; 32:19). He was also a great prophet. Long afterward it was remembered that "by a prophet the Lord brought Israel up from Egypt" (Hosea 12:13); and the promise of Moses for the future in Deuteronomy 18:15—"The Lord your God will raise up for you a prophet like me"— was claimed by the early Christians in application to Jesus Christ (Acts 3:22).

What is the difference between Moses and Pharaoh? What did Moses have that Pharaoh did not? Moses had a concern for human justice. Pharaoh enslaved a people. Moses liberated a people. Moses had a concern for human relations. Pharaoh ruled a people. Moses led a people. Moses had a knowledge of the will of God. Pharaoh was not unreligious. He was the beloved of Amon and the son of Re. But this relation gave him privilege. The knowledge of God which

came to Moses gave him a task and a service to render to his
fellow men.

What does Moses have that Pharaoh does not? Pharaoh has an
inevitably fading memory. Within his own lifetime the forces of
disintegration began to work in Egyptian history, and Egypt began
its long decline. The historian writes: "When Ramses II died, he had
not only outlived thirteen of his sons, but also, as it would appear,
the glory of his kingdom."[78] Great as were his material monuments,
they cannot but continue to crumble. Diodorus of Sicily (I, 47)
gives a description of what we call the Ramesseum, the mortuary
temple of Ramses II in western Thebes, with its colossal statues, and
records this inscription of the king, using the Greek form, Ozymandias, of his prenomen, User-maat-Re: "King of kings am I, Ozymandias. If anyone would know how great I am and where I lie,
let him surpass one of my works." Shelley took this up and wrote
of "Ozymandias":

> I met a traveller from an antique land
> Who said: Two vast and trunkless legs of stone
> Stand in the desert . . . Near them, on the sand,
> Half sunk, a shattered visage lies, whose frown,
> And wrinkled lip, and sneer of cold command,
> Tell that its sculptor well those passions read
> Which yet survive, stamped on these lifeless things,
> The hand that mocked them, and the heart that fed:
> And on the pedestal these words appear:
> "My name is Ozymandias, king of kings:
> Look on my works, ye Mighty, and despair!"
> Nothing beside remains. Round the decay
> Of that colossal wreck, boundless and bare
> The lone and level sands stretch far away.

The description is true, for in that temple today lie the shattered
pieces of the fallen colossus of Ramses II.[79]

But Moses has a growing influence in the world, for the passion
for justice and the powerful faith which he embodied will surely
continue to grow in the world.

# 3  THE PLAGUES OF EGYPT
## (Exodus 7-9)

In the two preceding chapters we have seen that in Egypt the children of Israel toiled in the house of bondage, and that Moses came forward to take their part against Pharaoh. At that juncture a remarkable series of disasters struck Egypt. In reference to these disasters, the word "plague" is used several times, as, for example, in Exodus 9:14; and the whole series is commonly known as the Ten Plagues or the Plagues of Egypt.

Does the account which is given of the plagues represent happenings which are physically possible? In 1906 Eduard Meyer expressed the opinion that the plagues are the free creations of the narrator.[1] In 1952 J. Coert Rylaarsdam set forth the still prevailing critical view in an analysis of the account of the plagues as having been put together artificially out of the three relatively late documents, J, E, and P. J tells of seven plagues, the fourth and fifth having been written up wholly by him. P has reworked five plagues, the third and sixth being by him alone and actually but duplicates of the fourth and fifth. E is to be recognized in five plagues, the ninth being entirely his. Thus no single tradition ever contained all ten plagues. The total account as we now have it is, moreover, very stylized and very repetitious. Although there probably were some actual events which facilitated the escape from Egypt, what we have here are "fantastic stories" and "a series of piously decorated accounts," the significance of which can only be symbolic rather than historical.[2]

For our part, we have already indicated, both with regard to the time of Abraham and with regard to the time of Moses, that the really important question would seem to us to be, not so much when

47

the hypothetical documents were put together into the form in which we have the materials, but rather whether what is thereby transmitted fits into the background of which it purports to tell. In the present case, therefore, our question is whether the account of the plagues fits the actual background of ancient Egypt and provides a coherent account of something that could actually have happened.

This is not to deny that the reports were passed down for a long time. Nor is it to deny that in the repeated telling, there was some expansion and embellishment of what was told. For example, in the contest between Moses and Aaron on the one side and Pharaoh and his magicians on the other, each side performed certain magical tricks. One does not know if Moses had time for something like this, or if this feature was added to make the story more interesting. Perhaps Moses and Aaron did have to meet their opponents on their own ground. At any rate the main trick is one which is actually known in Egyptian magic, and so it may come either from knowledge of what took place in the long contest, or from knowledge of Egyptian practices in general. We refer to the fact that, according to Exodus 7:9-12, both Aaron and the Egyptian magicians cast their rods to the ground and they became serpents. This is still done in Cairo today as a trick of magic. The Egyptian cobra can be paralyzed by putting pressure on a nerve in its neck. At a distance it is then readily mistaken for a cane. When the magician throws it on the ground, the jolt causes it to recover, and it crawls away.[3] But that Aaron's rod thereupon swallowed all the rest (Exodus 7:12) might seem, at least, to represent the touch of a storyteller.

In more significant matters there is a remarkable precision of reference to ancient Egypt. Because much in the account of the plagues has to do with the river, we may note the precisely correct way in which the river is referred to. The river is, of course, the great and famous river of Egypt. Ancient oracles declared that Egypt was the gift of the river and that those who drank of its water were Egyptians. This river we know as the Nile. This name comes from the Greeks who called it, using a word of unknown origin, the Nilus (*neilos*). The earliest to use the name is Hesiod (eighth century B.C.) who tells in his "Theogony" (338) of the god Oceanus and his wife Tethys, and writes:

> And Tethys bare to Ocean eddying rivers, Nilus. . . .

—and then goes on to name other famous rivers of the ancient world.

The Egyptians, however, used for the river the proper name Hapi (*ḥʿpi*). This name appears as early as in the Pyramid Texts, and since it occurs there in the form *ḥp* which means "to flow, to run," this may show the original derivation and meaning of the designation.[4] The river was also personified and deified, hence Hapi was also the name of the river as a god. As a river god Hapi was pictured as a bearded man with female breasts and hanging stomach to signify fertility, he was crowned with aquatic plants, and he held a tray of food or poured water from vases. He was praised in hymns such as the one preserved in Papyrus Sallier II, which speaks of the river as issuing from the earth and coming to keep Egypt alive.[5] The Old Testament did not believe in any river god such as that, so it never uses that name for the river.

But the Egyptians also used another word for the river. This likewise is found in the most ancient texts,[6] as well as in the Middle Kingdom and in the New Kingdom (that is, in the time with which we are now concerned), and it was in fact the everyday designation for the river. The word in question may be spelled *'itrw*, was probably modified in pronunciation to *iaru'ū*, and is finally found in Coptic as *iaro*.[7] It is at once evident that this is the word which is transcribed in Hebrew as *ye'or*. Ye'or occurs in the Old Testament for the first time in Genesis 41:1, where Pharaoh dreamed that he was standing by the river; next in Exodus 1:22, where the Hebrew children are to be cast into the river; and now at our present point of Exodus 7:17 and following, in the account of the plagues. This word is not a proper name like Hapi, but a common noun. It means "a channel for water, a stream of water, a river, the river," and in the plural (*ye'orim*) it is used (as in Exodus 7:19) for the irrigation canals leading off from the river. In the Greek translation of the Septuagint the word is properly rendered by the general Greek word for stream or river (*potamos*), and in the King James Version it is properly translated as "the river." It was, however, a specifically Egyptian word, as proper to use in regard to Egypt and as improper to use in regard to Palestine or Mesopotamia, as it is proper to use the word "bayou" in regard to Louisiana and improper to use it in regard to New England.

The Old Testament uses *ye'or* sixty-six times. In one passage (Daniel 12:5-7) where it occurs four times there is some doubt whether it refers to Egypt, but even here it may, since it follows immediately a prophecy relating to Egypt. In all the other more than sixty usages it refers unmistakably to Egypt. The Hebrew language of course has other words for stream or river, namely, *nahar* and *nakhal,* and these are used exclusively in all the Old Testament passages, both in the Pentateuch and elsewhere, which do *not* have to do with Egypt. Concerning this "exact discrimination" in the use of words, we may be inclined to agree with Melvin G. Kyle: "It is not art, but experience, that gives such skill in attending to so small a thing in so extensive use without a single mistake."[8]

Now we turn directly to the plagues themselves. We have indicated that the procedure which we would consider correct is to check the narrative, as far as possible, against the background of ancient Egypt from which it purports to come. If its essential features coincide at significant points with what is now known of ancient Egypt, we may consider that we are dealing with records based upon real happenings. In this case it so happens that a detailed investigation of the plagues has been made recently, which seems to represent this same general point of view. This study, by Greta Hort of Prague and of Aarhus University, Denmark, was published, in spite of its divergence from prevailing views, in the *Zeitschrift für die alttestamentliche Wissenschaft.*[9] In making the publication, the editors of the *Zeitschrift* explain that they have been assured by scientific authorities that the facts given in the fields of geology and microbiology are correct.[10] We will, accordingly, draw upon the facts set forth in this study in the following analysis of the happenings known as the ten plagues.

In the first plague (Exodus 7:14-25), the river was turned to blood; this affected all Egypt; and the phenomenon did not come to an abrupt cessation. As the water in the river, its canals, pools, and ponds, turned to blood, the fish in the river died, the water "stank" (Exodus 7:21, KJV), and the Egyptians dug round about the river for water to drink.

The Nile (using now the familiar name, derived from the Greek) is formed by the flowing together, at Khartoum, of two rivers. The White Nile rises in the lake country of East Africa, practically at the equator, and flows north through the swamps of the Sudan. The daily rains of the tropics provide a relatively constant and large flow of water. In so far as there is variation, the flow is smallest in April and largest in November. The Blue Nile rises in the mountains of Ethiopia and plunges swiftly down a steep gorge to its junction with the other river. At the sources of the Blue Nile the summer rains come at the same time as the maximum runoff from the snow fields. From low water in May to high in September, there is a tremendous increase in volume. There is also one tributary which joins the Nile one hundred and forty miles below Khartoum, namely, the Atbara. Since it also descends from the Ethiopian plateau its characteristics are similar to those of the Blue Nile, although it is a smaller stream. It may run dry in the winter; it reaches its highest water in September.

As to color, a glass of the water of the White Nile looks like a glass of ordinary drinking water to which a few drops of milk have been added. This coloration is due to the decomposed vegetable matter which has been picked up in the Sudan swamps. At its lowest time, it also carries fresh vegetable matter and attains a green color. During most of the year, the water of the Blue Nile is clear and beautiful and, as the name of the river suggests, looks blue. But the soil of the Ethiopian plateau where the Blue Nile and the Atbara rise, and of the gorges through which they descend, is typically a red earth. At the flood season a great deal of it is washed down, and the higher the rivers, the more is washed away. The more red sediment the streams carry, the redder their water appears. The Blue Nile also virtually dams off the White Nile at flood time, and its sediments, as well as those of the Atbara, carry all the way down to the Delta. Therefore, a very high inundation will explain the fact that the river of Egypt was turned, in graphic phrase, "to blood."

The red earth sediment will not, however, explain the other phenomena found in this plague. But in his recent work on hydrobotany, the German scientist, Gessner, has suggested that the high precipitation also brought down from mountain lakes a great mass of the algae known as flagellates, and their bacteria, and that these caused the death of the fish and the stench of the water.[11] Furthermore, the extra high inundation probably filled and broke in the wells; therefore, all the Egyptians could do to get potable water was to dig near the river (Exodus 7:24) and thus obtain water which was filtered through the earth.

From the time when the Blue Nile and Atbara are in flood, this plague must have come on in the late summer and early fall, and it was doubtless afflicting Egypt grievously in, say, August/September. It is readily understandable, too, that it affected all of Egypt, and that it did not end abruptly.

The second plague (Exodus 8:1-15=Hebrew text 7:26-8:11) was that of frogs; it affected all Egypt; it ceased abruptly. Frogs came out of the river and swarmed over the whole land. They suddenly died in the houses and fields. They were collected in heaps, and the land stank.

When the Nile begins to fall at the end of September/October, it is normal for the frogs to come out on the banks of the river. But Exodus 7:25 states that this was only seven days after the Lord had smitten the river; therefore, it was still in August/September. The explanation, accordingly, is that the mass death of the fish had polluted the normal habitat of the frogs, they were forced out of the river, and they sought out the houses and fields where they could find water and shelter from the sun. Let us suppose, also, that the masses of dead fish became points of origination for the spread of the *Bacillus anthracis,* which is carried by insects, and that the frogs were already infected when they came on land. This would account for the sudden death and rapid foul decomposition of the frogs.

The third plague (Exodus 8:16-19 = Hebrew text 8:12-15) was of mosquitoes; all Egypt was affected; the affliction did not stop abruptly.

The problem here is to identify the insect mentioned in Exodus 8:16, for the meaning of the Hebrew word (*kinnim*) which is used is not certain. The same word is used in the Talmud for "lice," and the King James Version gives this rendering; but the late meaning is not necessarily correct here. The word is translated in the Septuagint by the Greek word *sknips.* Some think this word means "gnats"; Philo (*Life of Moses* I, 108) describes the creatures as getting into the nostrils, ears, and eyes, which sounds like gnats; and this is the translation adopted in the Revised Standard Version. But two other words are available in Greek (*kōnōps* and *empis*) which mean "gnat"; and when Herodotus (II, 95) says that gnats are abundant in Egypt, he uses the former of these two words. Origen, who lived in Egypt, said in his *Homily on Exodus* that the creatures were small stinging insects, which would probably mean mosquitoes;[12] this explanation seems the most likely; it is adopted in the American Translation.

In Egypt mosquitoes become particularly numerous in October/November. In this year when the Nile was unusually high, it is very likely that the mosquitoes would be unusually numerous. They would be in all of Egypt, and the plague of them would subside only gradually.

The fourth plague (Exodus 8:20-32 = Hebrew text 8:16-28) was of flies; they were not in Goshen; the plague ceased abruptly. These flies filled the houses of Upper Egypt, but, having come suddenly, they also disappeared suddenly.

The ordinary fly is enough of a pest in Egypt, and is mentioned by the ordinary Hebrew word in Isaiah 7:18 as a symbol for Egypt; but in the present passage a different Hebrew word is used. There is a different kind of small fly which appears in Egypt in the spring; but we are now in the early winter. What is needed to correspond with the account is a fly which would multiply en masse under favorable circumstances; which would thus multiply in the tropical and subtropical regions of Upper Egypt but not in the more Mediterranean climate of Goshen; and which would transmit the skin disease of the sixth plague, yet to be mentioned. All of these conditions are fulfilled by the fly, *Stomoxys calcitrans*.

It may be supposed, therefore, that as the Nile receded breeding places became abundant for this fly. At that time, probably in November/December, there was a mass multiplication of the flies, coming suddenly, and ending suddenly too.

The fifth plague (Exodus 9:1-7) was that of a cattle pest; it did not affect the cattle of the Israelites; it did not cease abruptly. This fatal epidemic disease fell upon the Egyptian cattle which were in the field, upon the horses, asses, camels, herds, and flocks.

The statement in Exodus 9:6 that all the cattle died might appear to be inconsistent with the instruction in Exodus 9:19 to get the cattle under shelter; but it has already been made plain by Exodus 9:3 that it was only the cattle then out in the field which were affected by this plague. During the inundation, it may be supposed, the cattle were stabled; now, perhaps in December/January, some cattle were out in fields from which the water had withdrawn. Here in the fields, where the heaps of dead frogs had been piled (Exodus 8:14), the cattle, too, contracted the highly infectious and usually fatal anthrax. But in the north, in Goshen, the cattle were still stabled, and they escaped.

In the sixth plague (Exodus 9:8-12), both men and beasts were afflicted with boils and sores; this did not happen in Israel; nor did the plague cease abruptly.

The description of this plague fits anthrax very exactly, since this disease is characterized by ulcerations of the skin and the formation of malignant pustules. It affects chiefly the legs and feet, "blackleg" being a synonym of symptomatic anthrax. In the latter connection it may be noted that the Egyptian magicians are said to have been unable to "stand" before Moses (Exodus 9:11); and that the word for "boil" which is used here occurs also in Deuteronomy 28:35 where the boils are explicitly said to have affected the knees and the legs.

A principal transmitter of anthrax is *Stomoxys calcitrans,* identified above as the probable fly of the fourth plague; it bites both men and animals, and concentrates its attack upon the lower extremities. We may suppose, therefore, that it was by this agency that the anthrax which had already killed the frogs and then the cattle early in the field was now, perhaps at the end of December/January, carried not only to other cattle but to human beings as well.

The seventh plague (Exodus 9:13-35) was of hail; it did not fall in the land of Goshen; it came to an abrupt end. This tremendous hailstorm, accompanied by lightning and thunder, fell upon all men and animals in Upper Egypt who were not under shelter; it ruined the flax and barley, but not the wheat and spelt.

In Upper Egypt hailstorms can occur at any time of the year; in the Mediterranean climatic zone, including Goshen, they come in the summer but not in the winter. By the sequence of the plagues as thus far indicated, we are now in the winter, say January/February. In Egypt flax is normally sown at the beginning of January and is in flower three weeks later. Barley, normally sown in August, is harvested in February. With the high rise of the Nile, both were probably a little late and were exactly at the vulnerable point when the terrible hailstorm took place. Wheat and spelt, normally sown in August, are not harvested until toward the end of March; like the flax and barley, they too were probably a little late and were not yet at the point where maximum damage was done to them.

The eighth plague (Exodus 10:1-20) was of locusts; it affected all Egypt; it came to an end abruptly. An east wind blew all day and night and brought a dense swarm of locusts upon the land; they ate everything green that the hail had left; then a west wind drove them all into the sea.

In the fall locusts come from the Sudan to the regions around Port Sudan and Jidda and lay their eggs; during the winter the new generation hatches; in February/March they migrate to Palestine and Egypt, the prevailing winds affecting the way they go. A strong east wind would do exactly what Exodus says, bring the locusts in upon the land of Egypt. As for the west wind it is, in the Hebrew, literally a "sea wind." In Palestine a sea wind was a west wind; here in Egypt it would be more a northwest or north wind. Such a wind would, in fact, take the locusts out of the land.

The ninth plague (Exodus 10:21-29) was of darkness; it did not affect Israel; it ceased abruptly. This darkness continued for three days, and was such a thick darkness that people could not see one another.

In Egypt the khamsin is the hot southerly wind which comes in from the Sahara, carrying desert sand. It appears in Egypt from March to May; we are now, according to the sequence of the plagues, in early March/April. The khamsin normally blows for two or three days; three days is the duration of the present plague. It may be remembered that in this year a deep layer of red earth had been deposited over the land, and that there was now no vegetation to hold the soil in place, since the plant life had been destroyed by the hail and the locusts. So the sand and dust from the desert in addition to the red earth of Egypt, driven by the first khamsin of the year, produced an unprecedented obscuration of the atmosphere, and it was so dark that no one went out. But the people of Israel had light where they dwelt (as the Revised Standard Version correctly translates in verse 23). The Wadi Tumilat, running at right angles to the narrow Nile Valley, would be the region most likely to be protected from a khamsin from the south.

In the tenth plague (Exodus 11:1-12:33), death came to the first-born of men and animals among the Egyptians, but not in Israel. If we follow the same line of interpretation established above, we may assume a children's pestilence, bypassing Israel, but culminating in the death of the first-born son of the king of Egypt.[13] By the sequence of the plagues the date is now March/April.

From the foregoing facts we conclude that the biblical account of the plagues represents events which in their essential points would have been physically possible in ancient Egypt. In the investigation which we have now summarized, Greta Hort comes to the positive conclusion:

We have found that each of the plagues in its essential features describes correctly a natural phenomenon, which, though far from common, may yet happen in Egypt from time to time. Moreover, with the exception of plague no. 7 we have also found that each of the plagues follows directly or indirectly but always necessarily from the first plague and in the sequence described in the Bible. We have further found that the range and manner of cessation of each

plague coincide with that of the natural phenomenon described. . . .
These conclusions prove that the Bible gives us an historically accurate account of the ten plagues, and, unless we are willing to
credit E or some predecessor of his with a most intimate knowledge
of life in Egypt and with having transferred a series of events which
he himself had witnessed to Mosaic times, we must also conclude
that the Biblical account gives us true and historically accurate
information of the events which led up to the Exodus of Israel from
Egypt.[14]

If the account of the plagues of Egypt is physically possible, may
we also say that it is psychologically credible? An affirmative answer
may be given here more quickly. The psychological sequence of
events is as follows. Moses and Aaron ask Pharaoh to let the
Israelite people go, but his heart is hardened and he refuses to let
the people go (Exodus 7:14). The first plague strikes, and Pharaoh is
still obdurate (7:23). The second plague comes in swift succession
to the first; now Pharaoh relents and promises to let the people go
if only the visitation will cease (8:8). The second plague ceases
abruptly; then Pharaoh hardens his heart again (8:15). Pharaoh
then holds out in obduracy through another plague, the third, but
in the fourth he relents, only to harden his heart again when it
ceases (8:32). Through the fifth and sixth plagues the heart of the
king is still hard, in the seventh plague he relents, but when the hail
ceases abruptly he returns to his intransigence (9:35). In the
eighth plague he vacillates, promises freedom, then, when it ceases
abruptly, hardens his heart again (10:20). In the ninth plague he is
obdurate; in the tenth he makes the final capitulation, only to pursue
the people after they have departed.

In giving this narrative it is said sometimes that "Pharaoh . . .
hardened his heart" (e.g., 9:34), sometimes that his "heart . . . was
hardened" (e.g., 9:35), and sometimes that "the Lord hardened
Pharaoh's heart" (e.g., 10:27). These would appear to be just
different ways of stating the same fact and, among them, they give
clear recognition to the responsibility of Pharaoh as well as expression to the profound Israelite perception that in the last analysis all
that happens is under the control of God.

As for the repeated hardening of the heart of Pharaoh, this may
appear to be a feature of the stylized and repetitious character which
is often alleged against the narrative. But may this not rather point
to an underlying psychological fact which, unfortunately, is pro-
foundly true to human nature? Repentance and change of mind are

often found in the midst of disaster; they are often enough also forgotten when the trouble is past. Thus it was with Pharaoh; thus it is even until now. This account is, psychologically, only all too credible.

The account is, also, prophetically significant. The work of Moses in relation to these catastrophic events is not essentially that of a magician, although, as we have acknowledged, there may have been a slight tendency to expand the narrative in that direction. No, his work was essentially that of a prophet, and we have already noted, in the preceding chapter, the statement of Hosea 12:13 which explicitly attributes to Moses the function of a prophet. Moses was the first, but not the last, of that line of personages to whom this title properly attaches.[15] Here for the first time, but after this many times too, a common man stood against a king with words and signs of rebuke. The prophet sees, foresees, and sees into both natural and historical events and tells what God is doing in them. As Martin Buber puts it about the relation between the plague events in Egypt and the spoken words of Moses and Aaron: "Each of these events occurs between one prophetic utterance and the next, words of warning and words of interpretation."[16]

What is the warning? Is it not that even natural disaster may strike hard against a sinful man or nation?

What is the interpretation? Is it not that God is at work, to call those who are at enmity with him to repentance, and to set his people free?

At this point those who see the plagues as historical, as we do, and those who see them as symbolical, come again together. Here we are taught, as J. Coert Rylaarsdam states it, that "the living God of Israel . . . makes nature serve his purposes for man's fulfillment," and that "the living God . . . seeks men's allegiance and redemption."[17]

# 4 LET MY PEOPLE GO
## (*Exodus* 10-11)

Thus far we have seen that the children of Israel found Egypt to be a house of bondage, that Pharaoh and Moses confronted each other in an epic contest of wills, and that a series of unprecedented natural disasters fell upon Egypt as the conflict reached its height. In the consideration of these matters we have necessarily been involved in problems of detail: When were the Israelites in Egypt? Who was the pharaoh of the oppression? What took place in the plagues? But amidst the complexities of these investigations, we do not wish to lose sight of the most important part of the matter. Therefore we ask now: What was the essence of the exodus?

In the exodus the central fact was the setting free of the people from bondage. They were in physical bondage in forced labor, and in spiritual bondage in being unable to worship God as they wished. They obtained freedom. It was a physical freedom to go where they wished, and a spiritual freedom to worship God as they wished.

The request and claim for this freedom constituted the essential demand with which, on behalf of God, Moses faced Pharaoh. It is expressed in the four words which, during the long contest, ring out like a recurring refrain, ever more insistently: "Let my people go." We find the words at the following points: In Exodus 5:1 Moses and Aaron confront Pharaoh for the first time. They say: "Thus says the Lord, the God of Israel, 'Let my people go, that they may hold a feast to me in the wilderness.'" In Exodus 7:16, before the first plague in which the river was turned to blood, Moses is instructed to say to Pharaoh: "The Lord, the God of the Hebrews, sent me to you, saying, 'Let my people go, that they may serve me in the wilderness.'" In Exodus 8:1, before the second plague of frogs, Moses was told to say: "Thus says the Lord, 'Let my people go, that they may serve me.'" In Exodus 8:20, before the fourth plague of flies, Moses was charged to communicate to the king this statement: "Thus says the Lord, 'Let my people go, that they may serve me.'" In Exodus 9:1, before the fifth plague of cattle pest, Moses is told to say to the king: "Thus says the Lord, the God of the Hebrews, 'Let my people go, that they may serve me.'" In Exodus 9:13, before the seventh plague of hail, Moses is instructed to say: "Thus says the Lord, the God of the Hebrews, 'Let my people go, that they may serve me.'" In Exodus 10:3, before the eighth plague of locusts, Moses and Aaron said to Pharaoh: "Thus says the Lord, the God of the Hebrews, 'How long will you refuse to humble yourself before me? Let my people go, that they may serve me.'" That was the repeated and fundamental demand—"Let my people go!"

The essential happening in the exodus was the going forth of the Israelites from bondage to freedom. Not all students of the Bible agree about the solution of the detailed problems which we have taken up in the preceding chapters. Some doubt that the Israelites, or at any rate that all of them, were ever down in Egypt. Some minimize or eliminate the role of Moses. Some are skeptical concerning the historicity of the plagues. But there seems to be an increasing tendency to recognize that an event of deliverance actually took place and was of decisive importance. Eduard Meyer, for example, supposed that probably some Semitic tribes once wandered out of Egypt, but doubted that any Israelite tribes had anything to do with it; but over against that Rudolf Kittel insists that as far as the servitude is concerned, no people would have invented so ignominious and shameful an episode in its national history.[1] Martin Noth thinks it is impossible to say anything definite about the specific role and significance of Moses, but, concerning the deliverance of Israel from Egypt, he writes: "There can be no doubt, however, that this was a real event; we can discern to some extent the conditions and circumstances which led to it and can fit it into a historical situation of which we have quite reasonable knowledge."[2] J. Coert Rylaarsdam speaks of the stories of the plagues as "fantastic," but he regards the general outline of Israel's life and experience in Egypt and in the desert as in harmony with typical conditions in the Near East until recent times.[3] Bernhard W. Anderson, too, recognizes that the modern reader has difficulties with the story of the plagues, and thinks that in it there is a tendency to heighten the emphasis on miracles, but he also writes: "Nevertheless, Israel's ancient faith undoubtedly was based on the experience of actual events which facilitated the escape of slaves from Egypt, events in which they perceived in moments of faith the work of God."[4] That actual escape from slavery to freedom was the central happening in the exodus.

It was the same event upon which the remembrance of Israel focused ever afterward. The people of Israel never ceased to recall that they had been brought out of Egypt. Deuteronomy 26:7-8 records a formula which was often repeated: "And the Lord brought us out of Egypt with a mighty hand and an outstretched arm, with great terror, with signs and wonders." In Judges 6:13, Gideon tells how their fathers had often recounted: "Did not the Lord bring us up from Egypt?" In that event God delivered them from physical and spiritual bondage. He made them a free people, and he made them his people. Ever afterward the people of Israel were held together by their relation to that decisive event. So the book of Exodus, which records that event, has a place in the Old Testament which is comparable, as J. Coert Rylaarsdam points out, to that of the gospels in the New Testament. Here is narrated the historic happening on which the community of Israel was built, as in the gospels is unfolded the historic deed on which the church was built. Neither the New Testament church nor the Old Testament community of faith is held together simply by a common life or by common principles or practices. "It is held together," Rylaarsdam observes, "by the remembrance and celebration of the particular historical event which it affirms as the event of revelation. . . . In the Old Testament it is primarily the book of Exodus that provides, celebrates, and insists on this historical basis which is both the distinctive feature and the offense of the Bible and of Christian faith. Exodus serves especially as a shield which protects the biblical community from being swallowed up by some nonhistorical, universal system, whether mystical or rational. Exodus provides a record of the framework of faith. . . ."[5] That it is which constituted, ever afterward, the essential historical remembrance of the community.

If the essence of the ancient exodus, which is seen in the demand of Moses on Pharaoh, in the actual event, and in the never-ceasing remembrance thereof, was liberation from physical and spiritual bondage, we may next ask if there are examples of exodus in our time? Yes, there has been a modern exodus of the Jews as well as an ancient one. Persecution of this people has persisted. Why it has done so is an apparently inexplicable mystery, but it is an inescapable fact, as well as an unutterable tragedy. In ancient Egypt in 1300 B.C. an Egyptian, probably a taskmaster (cf. Exodus 3:7), was "beating a Hebrew" (Exodus 2:11); at the same time the minions of Pharaoh were casting into the river every son born to the Hebrews. In modern terms this was sadism, which is that love of cruelty manifest in the infliction of pain and torture; and genocide, which is the murder of a race, the extermination of a people. In Modern Europe in A.D. 1940, sadism and genocide were again being directed against the same people. In the Library of the Alliance Israélite Universelle there is a volume called the *Livre sans Nom,* "The Book without a Name." It was engraved by an anonymous artist who escaped from Auschwitz, the most notorious of Hitler's concentration camps. In his book on *Moses and the Vocation of the Jewish People,* André Neher has printed side by side some of these sketches and some of the paintings from ancient Egyptian tombs. In both, in appalling parallelism, human beings bend to their forced labor. Neher comments: "What brings Egypt and Auschwitz so close together is not only the fact that violence was done to the *same* people, but that it was in both places a carefully planned violence."[6]

At Auschwitz in the forced labor camps the inmates were underfed, worked to emaciation, given five hours of sleep a night on hard shelves, and subjected to every atrocity. At Birkenau, two miles from the main camp, gas chambers held three thousand persons at a time and exterminated ten thousand a day. Here Adolf Hitler and Adolf Eichmann concentrated their efforts for a "final solution" of the Jewish problem. Here, according to generally accepted figures, the Jewish death toll reached nearly a million Poles, 50,000 Germans, 100,000 Dutch, 150,000 French, 50,000 Austrians and Czechs, 50,000 Greeks, 250,000 Bulgarians, Italians, Yugoslavs, and Rumanians, and 250,000 Hungarians. In all the camps, an estimated six million Jews, including one million children, perished. The dimensions of this total horror exceed our comprehension; the significance of it for a single victim may perhaps be dimly apprehended. Something of what it meant to a young Jewish philosopher, Benjamin Fondane, is expressed in a poem which he did not have time to finish because the convoy took him to Auschwitz:

> 'Tis to you that I speak, ye men of the antipodes.
> I am speaking as a man to other men,
> With the little left in me of Man,

With the small voice remaining in my throat.
My blood o'erspills the roads. Would that it,
Would that it did not cry for vengeance!
The bugles blow. The beasts are cornered.
Let me speak to you with the same words
We had of old in common:
There are few you might understand.

The day will surely come, when all our thirst is
Slaked, and we shall be beyond the land of memory.
Death will have completed the labours of hate.
I shall be a handful of nettles beneath your feet.
Then . . . Well . . . Know that I had a face like yours;
A mouth that prayed like yours. . . .

Like you I have read all the papers and books,
And I knew nothing about the world,
And nothing about Man,
Although I often said I knew.

And when death, death came, perhaps
I pretended to know what it was; but truly,
I can tell you at this hour,
It entered fully into my astonished eyes,
Astonished that they understood so little
Did you understand more?

Yet no!
I was not a man like you.
You were not born on the road.
Nobody has thrown your little ones into the gutter,
Like little cats whose eyes are not yet open.
You have not wandered from town to town.
Hounded by the police;
You have not known the disaster at dawn,
The cattle trucks,
The bitter sobbing of humiliation—
Accused of a crime you did not commit—
The crime of existing—
You never changed your name or face
To rid yourself of the hue and cry . . .
A face they spat upon!

. . . When you examine this handful of nettles
Which was I in another century,
In a history which is lost to you,

Only remember that I was innocent;
And on that day like you, mortals,
I also had a face
Marked by anger, pity, joy,

Simply . . . the face of a Man.[7]

Nor was Europe in the 1940's the only place and time where ancient Egypt lived again in the experience of the Jews. In almost every country some version of the ghetto has sometime existed. Although the Muslim lands have never slaughtered the Jews as wantonly as have the Christian lands, there too from Yemen to Morocco are the *mellahs,* as the Oriental ghettos are called. And there in Morocco, for a single almost minor example lightly noted in the daily press of the world, at Mazaqan in 1955 the houses of five thousand Jews were burned.

But if persecution has persisted, so too have memory and hope. The memory of an ancient exodus and the hope for a modern one have never died. Benjamin Fondane entitled his poem, just quoted, "Exodus"; and in every land Jews have recalled the ancient story and pondered the prophecies. In fact, a modern exodus has actually taken place. When the Jew, Alfred Dreyfus, was condemned and mobs in the streets of Paris cried, "Death to the Jews," Theodor Herzl heard and could not forget. The idea of a Jewish state came to him. It seemed to him that only if Jews were again a nation in their own land, would all Jews of all lands be really free men. In 1897, as blood riots increased against Jews in Russia, Poland, Rumania, Austria, and Germany, as well as in France, a world convention of Jews met at Basle, Switzerland. They launched a movement which they called Zionism and defined in the statement: "The aim of Zionism is to create a homeland for the Jewish people in Palestine secured by public law." After the Romans destroyed their capital and temple in A.D. 70 and 135, most of the Jews were scattered in a vast dispersion all around the world. Yet some always continued to live in Palestine in settlements of varying extent all the way from Gaza and Hebron in the south to Tiberias and Safad in the north.[8] In all lands, too, the Jews continued to remember the holy land as the homeland. So, when there was persecution, at least some refugees tried to make their way back and, amidst the horrors of our times, the number to whom this appeared the only hope became very great. Therefore, fleeing by every desperate way they knew, back they went.

In the meantime, the Arabs under Muhammad's second successor, 'Umar, took Jerusalem in A.D. 638, and Palestine became largely an Arab land, and then a Turkish land. But the British defeated the Turks in 1917 and, after World War I, received a mandate to govern Palestine. When the British position was desperate during the war, the famous Balfour Declaration viewed with favor the establishment in Palestine of a national home for the Jewish people, and promised best endeavors to facilitate the accomplishment of this object. When the understandable opposition of the Arab world to the plan was realized, and the economic importance of favorable ties with the Arab world and its oil was recalled, many efforts were directed against the implementation of the project. In 1947, so that in at least a part of Palestine a state of Israel might exist, the United Nations voted for the partition of the land. In 1948 the mandate came to an end, the British left, and the state of Israel declared its independence. The Arab countries moved against the new state, but the Israelis stood alone and won by force of arms that which, as they saw it, had been given them legally by the conscience of the world.

The foregoing is, in brief, the history which has been woven into the powerful novel by Leon Uris, the title of which, like that of the poem by Benjamin Fondane, is *Exodus*.[9] In it, Dov Landau, a Jewish boy of Warsaw—ghetto rat, sewer rat, rubble rat—lives through the massacre of the Jews in Warsaw, survives Auschwitz, escapes the British detention camp on Cyprus, fights with the Jewish forces in Palestine and, as the book closes in mingled triumph and tragedy, reads the ritual of the celebration of passover in the free state of Israel. In that ritual, as will be seen in the next chapter, the question is asked:

Why is this night different from all other nights?

—and the answer is given that it is different because it celebrates the most important event in the history of the Jewish people, the event of their going forth in triumph from slavery into freedom.

That is the modern exodus. If we believe in the ancient one I think—with all possible consideration for the rights of the Arab world too—we should believe in and assist this modern one also.

The exodus of the colonial peoples is another modern example. In India the British colonial administration built roads and railroads, trained a civil service, and did work in agriculture and medicine, yet almost made it possible for Winston Churchill to say in England, as he tried to hold onto this prize, that India was England's daily bread—while the millions of India did not yet have their own daily bread. It was a great day in the history of human freedom, therefore, when at last, overcome by Gandhi's strange method of nonviolence, the British marched away and when, in 1950, the new constitution of a sovereign democratic republic undertook to secure for all people of India

Justice, social, economic and political;
Liberty of thought, expression, belief, faith and worship;
Equality of status and opportunity; and . . .
Fraternity assuring the dignity of the individual and the unity of the Nation.

Elsewhere in the world, many other countries have come into freedom. In 1960 there were twenty-seven states in Africa which had become independent. The first of the newly self-governing units was Ghana. This state (from whence comes half the chocolate of the world) links itself with the empire of Ghana which flourished in West Central Africa around A.D. 800. In the Eighteenth century, two and a half million slaves were taken from the area. For a century, the British ruled. Then Kwame Nkrumah spent ten years in the United States, worked his way through Lincoln University in Pennsylvania, and back at home formed a people's party to act in civil disobedience and take positive action for independence. The British put him in jail, then released him to be prime minister after he obtained a large majority of votes in a 1951 election following the granting of a new constitution. In the United Nations, Nkrumah has declared, as quoted in the press: "The existence of a strong group of neutral nations cannot fail to strengthen this world assembly."

The Congo has recently been most prominently in the eyes of the world. About the time Columbus discovered America, the Portuguese began a slave trade in this region which lasted one hundred and fifty years and took one and a half million slaves. After that King Leopold II of Belgium took the area for what has been called virtually a vast private estate. On the rubber plantations the native workers were brutally exploited. John Gunther estimates that eight million Africans were killed. In 1908 the Congo became a colony. In 1960—illy prepared, with no African lawyers, doctors, or engineers, and only sixteen college graduates—it became free, to the accompaniment of terror and violence, and faced a future that was far from clear.

Yet with all the terror and trouble, we cannot ask the peoples who are moving toward freedom to turn back on that road. Theirs, too, is an exodus and, if we believe in the ancient exodus, I think we should believe in these modern ones as well, and try to help.

There is also an exodus of the Negro people in the United States of America. Theirs has been a notable movement up from slavery, but a movement which, even here, is yet far short of its proper goals. On the way, with a kinship of experience with the ancient Israelites, they have put the inmost meaning of the story of Moses and the exodus into their spiritual song:

> Go down, Moses,
> Way down in Egypt land,
> Tell ole Pharaoh,
> Let my people go.

In this connection, it may not be amiss to recall that Moses himself, according to Numbers 12:1, married a Cushite woman, and that of course means that he had a Negro wife.

So, if we believe in the ancient exodus, I think we should believe in the exodus of the Negro people from the land of oppression, and help them too.

What, then, are the elements in a real exodus? According to Exodus 3:9, it was God who heard the cry and saw the oppression of his people. Therefore, in the last analysis, it is God whose purpose and intention it is that men should be free. In Exodus, too, it is people in whom—no matter how oppressed and how lacking in opportunity they are—there is still some spark of freedom's light, some desire to be free and to have what freedom means. God—even if sometimes he is not recognized—and people—even if sometimes they are pitifully confused and badly mistaken: these are the indispensable elements in every exodus. Therefore, if any exodus is really to succeed, the people who become free must also become the people of God. "Let my people go" was only one part of what God said; "that they may serve me" was the other part of what he said. If poor, ignorant, and misguided folk become free and then use their freedom as occasion for new injustice against their fellows, they have not yet made any true exodus. They must yet learn to be God's true people. "Let my people go," says the Lord God, "that they may serve me." Until they do that they have not found real freedom. It is the business of the church, therefore, in all lands, to help men become free physically and also spiritually—for only then will exodus be really accomplished.

# 5 PASSOVER!

## (Exodus 12:1-13:16)

On the eye of their departure from Egypt, the children of Israel ate a special meal. For the meal they had roast lamb and unleavened bread; at the same time with the blood of the lambs a mark was put on the doorposts of their houses. This event is recorded in the twelfth chapter of Exodus, where verses 1-13 outline the entire happening with special emphasis on the roast lamb; verses 14-20 tell more about the unleavened bread; and verses 21-27 tell more about the putting of the mark of blood on the doorposts. In verses 11, 21, and 27 it is stated that the name of the observance was "passover."

There is a widespread opinion among critical scholars that this account is an etiological legend, which means a story which attempts to assign a cause for something. The Jews certainly had a festival called passover at a later date; this story gives the festival an imaginary origin in the time of Moses—such is the theory. In accordance with the method we have already established, we will try to see the record against the background of the time and place from which it is supposed to have come, and see if it fits that background. To do this we will simply ask, Why did the children of Israel eat that meal in the land of Egypt on the eve of their departure?

In general the meal may have been familiar at that time and in that area. Many think that the oldest part of the account is found in 12:21-27, and this begins: "Then Moses called all the elders of Israel, and said to them, 'Select lambs for yourselves according to your families, and kill the passover lamb.'" That sounds as if Moses were speaking of something the people already knew about. The

Israelites were a shepherd people. They came into Egypt bringing their flocks and herds (Genesis 46:32), and that is why they were located in the land of Goshen (Genesis 46:34), which was an appropriate region for such a people. Among the shepherd people of the Near East ideas similar to those of the passover are so widespread that we may readily suppose that they go far back, and that the Israelites were following ancient shepherd customs in this meal. Note the following points:

The time was spring. We have already traced the sequence of the plagues in Egypt from late one summer (the first plague in August/September) to the next spring (the tenth plague in March/April). Exodus 13:4 names the month Abib, a Hebrew word meaning a "fresh ear" of corn and referring to the time when the barley shoots into ear. Exodus 12:2 calls it the first month of the year, which is what it was in the later calendar when the year began in the spring. In that calendar, which was derived from Babylonia, the name of the month was Nisan. In the old Arab calendar the corresponding month was Rajab, the seventh month reckoning from a beginning of the year in the autumn, and was a period of sacrifice. Indeed, the beginning of spring has been very widely regarded as a sacred season among the Arabs, the North Semites, and others.[1] The fact, therefore, that the time was spring and in particular the month Abib, which was equivalent to Nisan and to Rajab and to our March/April, suggests the possibility of a relationship of the passover to a more widespread shepherds' sacrificial observance of the springtime.

In the passover sacrifice a lamb was slain and eaten. According to Exodus 12:5, the lamb was a year old. The Hebrew is literally "the son of a year," and we might call it a yearling, one of those born in the preceding spring. It was probably not only a yearling but also a firstling, for Exodus 13 proceeds immediately to tell about the consecration of the first-born to the Lord; and Deuteronomy 15:20 says of the firstling of flock and herd: "You shall eat it, you and your household, before the Lord your God year by year"—and then goes on in Chapter 16 to tell of the passover. Early in the present century, Antonin Jaussen traveled among the Arabs in the land of Moab and wrote of their customs. He tells how among them the first-born of a flock of goats or sheep is considered sacred, marked, consecrated to a local deity, but kept for some special occasion, perhaps the presence of an important guest, and then eaten by the strangers and the family together.[2]

Unleavened bread was eaten. This has been the bread of the nomadic and seminomadic people of the Near East for thousands of years. It is what Abraham had Sarah bake for the visitors who came to his tent, when he asked her to get fine meal, and knead it, and make cakes (Genesis 18:6). Early in the nineteenth century John Lewis Burckhardt lived among the Bedouins of Sinai and Arabia and, in his report on this experience, he tells of their unleavened bread baked on hot stones.[3]

The blood of the sacrifice was put on the doorposts and lintels of the dwellings. Around 1900 Samuel I. Curtiss traveled in Syria, Palestine, and the Sinaitic Peninsula. In southern Palestine he was welcomed at the tent of an Arab. A goat was slain and some of the blood put on one of the tent cords. A woman explained that it was "for a blessing." In the Druse Mountains he saw blood marks on the lintel and doorposts of a shrine.[4]

These items of parallelism seem sufficient to make it probable that we are in fact, both in the biblical narrative and in these more recent survivals, in touch with ancient and widespread Semitic customs. These customs included the annual dedication and marking of the first-born of the flocks; the use of these animals in the following springtime for a festival meal; the eating of unleavened bread along with the meat; at the same time the marking of the dwellings with blood for protection and blessing. These were the elements of the ancient shepherds' meal which Moses had his people eat that memorable spring in Egypt, on the eve of their departure from the land. Perhaps they had been planning on the observance all along. Repeatedly, they had asked Pharaoh for permission to go three days' journey into the wilderness and sacrifice to the Lord; and in Exodus 34:25 the passover is called a *hag* or pilgrimage.

In general, then, the passover of the Israelites may have had the features of a meal which was otherwise known among the Semites of the ancient Near East. But in particular, as circumstances had developed, this meal had special purposes. For one thing, it had the very simple and obvious purpose of providing food. On the eve of a major adventure the best possible repast is often provided. These people were about to start for the desolate wilderness. Although they did not know it, many years of wandering and walking were ahead of them. The best meal they could have before they started was none too good.

Another purpose was to provide and establish fellowship. They ate by families; if one household was too small for a lamb, then a

man and his neighbor joined together (Exodus 12:4). Also, all the
families were doing the same thing at the same time, each with a
mark on its door which showed that all belonged together. To eat
together has been, all over the world, a way to establish kinship
or alliance. When Melchizedek made a treaty with Abraham, he
brought out bread and wine (Genesis 14:18). When Abimelech
made a covenant with Isaac, he made a feast and they ate and drank
(Genesis 26:30). To this day, to eat the food of an Arab is to be
entitled to his care and protection. In fact, a meal could mean an
alliance not only among people but also between them and their
God. When the Israelites met Jethro in the wilderness, the elders
of Israel ate bread with Moses' father-in-law "before God" (Exodus
18:12). Their table was spread in the presence of the Lord. Therefore, it could have been in the purpose of the passover not only to
fortify the people on the eve of departure on their great adventure,
but also to bind them together anew with one another and with
their God.

It could also have been the purpose to suggest and increase fearlessness. As a part of the observance, the protective mark was put
on the doors. As the great disasters struck Egypt, some came upon
the whole land, others spared the land of Goshen. The climax of
all was now at hand. One might well fear how it might fall. But
from ancient times, probably, a blood mark upon the door had
meant blessing and protection. So they used it now in faith and
hope. Whether the meal had been called passover before this, or
whether Moses introduced the name, is difficult to make out; but it
is possible that the name is connected with the significance just
indicated. The meaning of the name (*pesah*) is also difficult to make
out, but it seems to occur in the name of the city Tiphsah on the
Euphrates (I Kings 4:24). This is probably the Thapsacus where
Cyrus forded the river, finding it only breast high;[5] accordingly, the
word has to do with crossing or passing. The same root also appears
in a verbal form in Isaiah 31:5, which reads in the King James
Version: "As birds flying, so will the Lord of hosts defend Jerusalem;
defending also he will deliver it; and passing over he will preserve
it." So the deeper meaning is that of a "passing over" to preserve
and rescue.[6] While the blow falls upon the land, the Lord passes
over the houses of his people, as birds flying, to protect and deliver.

This, then, is why they ate the meal. Moses wanted to fortify his
people with good food on the eve of a great adventure, he wanted
to forge the bonds of their fellowship with each other and God,

he wanted to fill them with fearlessness in the assurance that, as birds flying, the Lord was hovering over to protect and preserve. In his book on *Moses,* Martin Buber also repudiates the explanation of the account of the passover as an etiological legend, maintains a historical approach, and reconstructs the situation as follows:

Favourable circumstances have, within a relatively brief period, provided a man possessing the character and destiny of a leader with the external prerequisites for the fulfillment of his immediate task, the leading of a group of semi-nomadic tribes out of a land of "bondage." The geographical and political conditions under which the impending wandering has to take place are tremendously difficult, no matter whether that wandering already aims at landed possession and settlement or, for the time being, at the resumption of a nomadic life. The human groups whom he proposes to lead out are only loosely associated with one another; their traditions have grown faint, their customs degenerate, their religious association insecure. The great thought of the man, his great impulse, is to establish a covenant of the tribes in the purer and freer atmosphere of the desert, which had once purified and freed him himself, and to establish that covenant on the basis of their common covenant with a common divinity who had been neglected for generations. However, the degree of inner unity is insufficient even for the way to this initial goal. The extraordinary events, to be sure, had their effect; but the sense of unity, unity of destiny and of road to be taken, was not yet ripe enough. At such times, as we find at all historical periods, what is required is a common symbolic act in which the joint existence is converted into a sensory experience. But this cannot be brought about of set purpose; any astutely calculated steps injure the basic root of eventuation. Even though promoted by the words and deeds of a man, it must evolve out of whatever has existed from times immemorial. And so Moses reintroduces the holy and ancient shepherds' meal, renewed in meaning and form.[7]

We have given an answer to the question as to why the children of Israel ate a special meal in Egypt before they left the land. We must now consider the further questions, How and why did they keep on eating the passover meal? It is to be noted that the Israelite people did continue the meal, and have continued it until today. The account in Exodus has the instruction that this should be done: "You shall observe this rite as an ordinance for you and for your sons for ever. And when you come to the land which the Lord will give you, as he has promised, you shall keep this service" (Exodus 12:24-25).

In Palestine the greatest change made was that whereas the passover had been a family festival observed in the homes, as we have seen, the effort was made to tie it to an official place of celebration. The Samaritans (who claim to be descendants of Ephraim and Manasseh, the sons of Joseph, and who claim that their priests are of the house of Levi through Aaron, Eleazar, and Phinehas) hold that six years after the entrance of the children of Israel into the promised land, Joshua built the tabernacle upon Mount Gerizim, and that that is, accordingly, the proper and only place for passover. This idea is tenaciously maintained by the remnant of Samaritans, now but two hundred in number, who still reside in Nablus at the foot of Mount Gerizim and every spring go up on the mountain to slaughter the lambs in the ancient rite.[8]

The book of Deuteronomy stated a different requirement: "And you shall offer the passover sacrifice to the Lord your God, from the flock or the herd, at the place which the Lord will choose, to make his name dwell there. . . . You may not offer the passover sacrifice within any of your towns which the Lord your God gives you; but at the place which the Lord your God will choose, to make his name dwell in it, there you shall offer the passover sacrifice" (Deuteronomy 16:2, 5). This, of course, pointed to Jerusalem and the temple. But the temple suffered destruction in 587 B.C. and, after that, priestly regulations probably again allowed for home observance.[9] In New Testament times there was emphasis again upon observance of the ceremony at Jerusalem (Luke 2:41), with slaughter of the lambs in the courts of the temple.[10] But after the temple underwent final destruction in A.D. 70 and 135, only home observance was possible.

So today that which is still continued is essentially a home ceremony. This is called the Seder, meaning "order of service," and it takes the place of the actual animal sacrifice and the ancient passover meal. According to the biblical date (Exodus 12:6, 8) the lamb was slain on the 14th day of Nisan, the first month of the spring, and the feast was eaten that night, which, with the new day beginning at sundown, would be the 15th of Nisan. In 1961, according to the Jewish calendar, the passover began at sundown on Friday, March 31. On the evening preceding the Seder, the master of the house makes a symbolic search for any leaven, and declares in Aramaic: "All leaven, whether detected or undetected, is hereby regarded as nonexistent or as mere dust of the earth." On the evening of the service proper, two candles burn in the home, and the following elements are on the Seder table: three cakes of matzoth, or unleavened bread; bitter herbs, such as horseradish, in memory of the bitter servitude of the past; a mixture of apples, nuts, raisins, and cinnamon, called haroseth, and considered symbolic of the mortar of the building work in Egypt; the roasted shankbone of a lamb, symbolizing the passover lamb; a roasted egg, probably derived from paganism, suggesting the new life of the springtime, and itself the source of the Easter egg of Christian custom; parsley or radishes, the relishes of an ancient banquet. In addition, four cups of wine mark the four promises of the Lord in Exodus 6:6-7: "I will bring you out"; "I will deliver you from their bondage"; "I will redeem you"; "I will take you for my people"; and in the center of the table a large goblet waits for Elijah, who is believed to come as the forerunner of the Messiah.

The foregoing explains how the passover observance has been carried on through the years; now we ask why it has been continued. The fundamental reason for its continuance, we believe, is because biblical religion is historical religion. If we are correct about the background of the passover, it was derived from an ancient shepherds' meal. That meal was essentially a nature festival of the springtime. In the springtime, a wandering shepherd people began to move from its winter quarters to summer grazing lands. In this festival they expressed the hope for protection on their way, and for good increase of their flocks and herds. So the festival reflected the rhythmic course of the shepherds' life, ever in close touch, as it was, with the cycles of nature.

Such a festival might surely have been left behind when that kind of life was largely left behind by the Israelites as they settled in the promised land, and also by many of their descendants who live in great cities all around the world. But wherever this people has gone, the festival of the passover has never been forgotten. Because Moses, as we believe, transformed the ancient nature festival into a historical festival, from his time on the meal has celebrated primarily a great historical event, namely, the event in which the Lord delivered the children of Israel from Egypt and made them his own people. Thus Exodus 12:26-27 instructs that when the children ask what the service means, they are to be told that "it is the sacrifice of the Lord's passover," and they are to be told what the Lord did for the people of Israel in Egypt.

In its main outline, the Seder begins with the Kiddush or sancti-
fication, in which the leader blesses God for having given this day
of the feast of unleavened bread as a memorial of the departure
from Egypt, and all drink the first cup. Then the leader breaks a
cake of unleavened bread and invites all who are hungry to come
and eat, and all who are in need to come and celebrate the passover.
He goes on: "At present we celebrate it here, but the next year we
hope to celebrate it in the land of Israel. This year, we are slaves
here, but the next year we hope to be free men." Thereupon the
youngest person asks: "Why is this night different from all other
nights?" That question introduces the Haggadah, which is the ex-
planatory narrative. The leader answers with Deuteronomy 6:21,
"We were Pharaoh's slaves in Egypt, and the Lord brought us out";
and then goes on to say that even if all present were scholars
who knew the law very well, it would still be incumbent upon them
to talk about the departure from Egypt. To elaborate the answer,
four imaginary sons are introduced—one wise, one wicked, one
simple, and one too young to phrase an interrogation—and it is
shown what teaching could be given to each one.

Next the leader uses what must once have been an alternate beginning of the Haggadah, as he quotes Joshua 24:2 and recalls that
the ancestors of the Israelites were anciently idolators. Then he cites
the promise of God to Abraham and, as he lifts the cup, summa-
rizes the whole history of the people in this statement: "And it is this
same promise which has been the support of our ancestors, and of
us also: for not one only has risen up against us, but in every generation there are some who rise up against us, to annihilate us; but
the Most High, blessed be he, has delivered us out of their hand."
As the chief example of such deliverance he then turns again to the
narrative of the bondage in Egypt and the escape from it. When he
enumerates the plagues, the leader dips his finger into the wine cup
and sprinkles a few drops, just as long ago the blood was sprinkled
to ward off evil. When he mentions the deliverance, a "litany of
wonders" is used to tell of the cumulative benefits experienced.
"What abundant favors the Omnipresent has conferred on us!" ex-
claims the leader, and goes on to recall that God not only brought
them out of Egypt, but also punished the Egyptians; not only
divided the sea, but also caused them to pass through on dry land;
not only led them to Mount Sinai, but also gave the law; not only
gave the law, but also brought them to the promised land; and not
only brought them to the promised land, but also built the temple. As

each successive benefit is cited, all present cry, *Dayyenu,* "It alone would have been sufficient." Finally, after further recital and explanation, the service moves into the Hallel, the chanting of Psalms 113-118. Psalm 113 begins, "Hallelujah!" that is, "Praise the Lord!" Psalm 114 recalls: "When Israel went forth from Egypt . . . the sea looked and fled." Psalm 118 exhorts: "O give thanks to the Lord, for he is good." Such is the historical ceremony of the Jewish passover, which makes present the ancient historical event and binds this people together with that which God has done in its history.[11]

Why do we ourselves, if we are members of the Christian faith and not of the Jewish, still think about the passover and still have reason to think about it? We have reason to ponder it because of its intrinsic values. There is a linear character about passover. It not only memorializes the deliverance of the children of Israel long ago from the power of Pharaoh; it also stands for their repeated deliverances down through the years, in every generation, and unto the present. It not only speaks of the liberty the Israelites got long ago, but also of the liberty they have had to strive for so many times ever since. Past and present merge here into one. As they tell about the ancient deliverance, even the modern Jews find themselves saying, in the Seder, "He brought *us* forth from Egypt," "He fed *us* with manna." There is, in fact, one passage in the ritual which says explicitly: "It is incumbent on every Israelite, in every generation, to look upon himself as if he had actually gone forth from Egypt. . . . It was not only our ancestors that the Most Holy redeemed from Egypt, but us also did he redeem with them."

There is an extensive quality about passover. It is, of course, an observance of Judaism, yet to some extent its meaning belongs to everybody. The freedom the Israelites wanted is the freedom all men want. To celebrate the freedom they once obtained is to celebrate all freedom that all men have ever gotten and will ever get. Discussing the passover, Theodor H. Gaster writes: "Whenever the trumpets sound in history, they sound for all ages; and when the bell tolls, the echo lives on forever."[12] And, we may add, the sound and the echo are for all men wherever there is the desire for freedom.

Furthermore, there is a depth of meaning about passover. It reminds us that the Israelites became really free, not only by escaping from bondage in Egypt, but also by accepting the law of God in the wilderness. They not only became free from servitude to Pharaoh, but also free to obey God, and only in obedience to God did they find true freedom. In the event of the exodus, God not only made a people free but also made them his people, and they made him their God. "On the broad human plane," writes Gaster of the passover, "it celebrates the attainment of freedom and of the vision of God: man casts aside his idols and repudiates his ignorance and obscurantism, and in that very act God reveals His presence and imparts knowledge."[13]

In addition to its intrinsic values, passover also has transmitted values. Passover has entered into the history and meaning of Christianity. When Jesus was on the way up to Jerusalem for the last time he spoke, according to the literal Greek of Luke 9:31, of the "exodus" which he was to accomplish there. In Jerusalem, according to Mark 14:12, the disciples asked him where they should prepare the passover. In the last supper which Jesus ate with the disciples, whether it was on or shortly before the exact passover day of orthodox Judaism, there were certainly features such as those we have seen in the description of the passover. The saying of a blessing and the drinking of a cup, the breaking of bread, and the hymn singing (as the Greek says literally in Mark 14:26) at the end, correspond to the features of the Seder even today, from the Kiddush to the Hallel, as we have just seen. So the passover of Moses entered into the last supper of Jesus, and the last supper of Jesus has become the evermore repeated Lord's Supper of the Christian Church. This, too, has to do with freedom, for it is written in John 8:36, "if the Son makes you free, you will be free indeed."

# 6  THROUGH THE SEA
## (Exodus 13:17-15:21)

When we come to the actual going forth of the children of Israel from the land of Egypt we again find the more critical students of the Old Testament dubious about the details of the narrative. Even among them there is an increasing tendency, to be sure, to recognize that there were once some Israelities in Egypt and that they actually made an exodus from there. But it is still often held that the different sources in the book of Exodus represent different views of the event and that, accordingly, we cannot tell what really happened. We have already seen that Martin Noth, for example, regards the exodus as a "real event" which we can fit "into a historical situation of which we have quite reasonable knowledge"; he also holds that the "incident certainly occurred on the eastern border of the delta" (a not unreasonable thought, inasmuch as that is the only way to get out of Egypt by land in the direction of Palestine), but as to more exact information he says: "It is impossible to ascertain the locality of the incident more precisely." He also states that our lack of knowledge about the localization of what transpired is at least partly responsible for the mystery and obscurity in which the event remains for us. He concludes: "The incident itself, which the Israelites experienced as an unexpected and mighty act of deliverance of their God, remains veiled from our sight."[1]

Assuredly, the deeper meaning of the event, as an act of God for the deliverance of his people, is veiled in the mystery which surrounds every divine act, into which only the eyes of faith can see. But since, as Noth observes, our knowledge or lack of knowledge of the localization of the events has much to do with our understanding of what happened, we will not hesitate to consider some of the details of where the Israelites were and went. Although here as elsewhere different sources may be involved, our attempt will continue to be to see if the narrative as a whole is consistent and intelligible (at least as far as information is available) in relation to the background of its time; if it is we shall also not hesitate to consider that here as elsewhere there are dependable records of what happened.

We turn, then, to the path of the Israelites. In this regard the Old Testament gives: (1) the general direction in which they went; (2) several stages and stopping points on the way. Critical theory, as alluded to above, generally holds that (1) and (2) do not agree. Let us look first at the general direction in which the children of Israel are said to have gone. Exodus 13:17-18 states: "When Pharaoh let the people go, God did not lead them by way of the land of the Philistines, although that was near; for God said, 'Lest the people repent when they see war, and return to Egypt.' But God led the people round by the way of the wilderness toward the Red Sea." As that says with complete accuracy, there are in general just two ways to go from Egypt to Palestine by land. One is up the coast, a way I once traversed by railroad; the other is out across the peninsula of Sinai, a way I have recently gone by air. We will describe these ways in turn.

Here is the coast route. From the delta of Egypt there is a strip of fertile land (mentioned already in our first chapter) which runs northeastward toward what is now the northern part of the Suez Canal. This extends from the present Zagazig (forty miles northeast of Cairo) to Kantarah on the Suez Canal. In ancient times the Pelusiac arm of the Nile flowed this way and went on to empty into the Mediterranean near Pelusium (Tell Farama, east of Port Said). The railroad which goes to Palestine begins at Kantarah and runs up along the coast. The ancient caravan and military route went the same way. The route began at the Egyptian city and fortress known as Thel (later Sile) (mentioned above in our second chapter), which has been identified with Tell Abu Seifeh, a mile and a half east of Kantarah. This is probably also the same as the "Fortress of the 'Ways [of Horus]'" mentioned in Papyrus Anastasi I (late Nineteenth Dynasty); and the same as the halting place "Ways of Horus" named in the story of Sinuhe (Twelfth Dynasty). The entire route was also probably called the Way of Horus: Horus (as we have seen above in our second chapter) was the chief god here in northeastern Egypt; and Pharaoh, the living embodiment of Horus, went this way on his victorious marches.

From Thel the coast route went out past the large seacoast lake now named Lake Bardawil (*sabkhat el-bardawil*) from the Crusader King Baldwin, and in Hellenistic and Roman times called the Sirbonian Sea. This lake is forty-five miles long and thirteen miles wide, and is separated from the Mediterranean Sea by only a narrow spit of land. The main route skirts the lake on the south or landward side. An alternate route runs along the narrow ridge of land between the lake and the sea, and is dangerous because of quicksand and the risk of submergence by a north wind. Thereafter the coast route proceeds across the Wadi el-'Arish, often considered the extreme frontier of Egypt, and goes on to Raphia (or Rafa) and to Gaza. The total distance from Kantarah to Gaza is one hundred and forty miles. Except for wells, the route traverses a waterless desert marked by low scrub growth and occasional groves of palm trees.

About A.D. 68 the Roman general Titus marched up this way. Josephus gives his itinerary as including these points: Tanis (by our identifications, the ancient city of Raamses and the modern San el-Hagar), Heracleopolis (probably now under the waters of Lake Menzaleh), Pelusium (Tell Farama), the temple of Casian Zeus (of which more later), Ostracine (unidentified), Rhinocorura (at Wadi el-'Arish), Raphia, and Gaza.[2] Assuming that these are day's marches, the trip evidently took about a week. In his time, the army of Thutmose III covered the distance in some ten days.[3]

On the exterior north wall of the great hypostyle hall of the temple at Karnak there is a representation of this route. It is a carving by Seti I, father and predecessor of Ramses II. It depicts in long sweep and large size military exploits of the Pharaoh, while beneath the feet of his horses and the wheels of his chariots, in much smaller scale, is a line of fortresses and sheets of water or lakes. The accompanying inscription gives the date as the first year of the king, and states that the campaign was against the Shoshu-land. The Shoshu were "wanderers," and the work probably refers to the Semites as nomads and pastoral people. The inscription describes the route as "starting from the fortress of Thel, to the Canaan." As far as we know, this is the earliest equivalent of a map from ancient Egypt. Telling of the carving, Alan H. Gardiner describes "the figures of the subservient Egyptians welcoming home the victorious Pharaoh thronged by hosts of prisoners, the battle-scene where the routed enemy is being trampled beneath the hooves of Pharaoh's horses, and the picture of Seti receiving the spoils of gold and silver amid a crowd of cringing Semites"; and declares that there can be little or no doubt but that this road from Kantarah to Gaza via Raphia "has witnessed the marches of nine-tenths of the armies that have sought to invade Palestine from Egypt, or Egypt from Palestine, along the land-route."[4]

This, then, was one way from Egypt to Palestine, namely, the coast route. Exodus 13:17 refers to this way: "God did not lead them by the [KJV] way of the land of the Philistines, although that was near; for God said, 'Lest the people repent when they see war, and return to Egypt.'" This passage says four things about the route. (1) As to name, the route is called the way of the land of the Philistines." As far as we know, the Philistines first settled in the coastal plain around 1175 B.C., a hundred years, by our reckoning, after the time of the exodus. The Philistines were so prominent that from then on this region was known as their land and, in fact, all of Palestine derived its name from them. From not long after the exodus and onward it was, therefore, natural to refer to this route across the coastal plain as "the way of the land of the Philistines." (2) As to convenience, this way was "near." The distance from the city of Raamses (San el-Hagar) to Thel (Tell Abu Seifeh) is only twenty-five miles; from there to Gaza was a journey of only a week or ten days. (3) As to the character of the route, here the people would "see war." For the scenes of war they were only too likely to witness along this way, we have but to recur to the carving on the Karnak temple, described above. (4) As to the usage of this route by the Israelites, "God did not lead them" by that way.

In spite of the clear correspondence between the biblical statement and what we otherwise know about this route, and in spite of the inherent probability that this route would be avoided for the very reason which the Bible gives, a currently favored critical theory supposes that this is the way which was taken. This theory was proposed by Otto Eissfeldt,[5] and has been accepted, among others, by Georg Beer,[6] H. Cazelles,[7] and Martin Noth.[8] The theory holds that Exodus 13:17-18 is from an author who had no concrete knowledge of the place of the exodus; that Exodus 14:2, although also late, is more specific and may even be accurate; and that, as far as they go, the references in Exodus 14:2 point to places near the beginning of the coast route, hence show that the Israelites actually went that way, in flat contradiction to Exodus 13:17-18.

In particular, the Baal-zephon of Exodus 14:2 is held, in this theory, to have been in the vicinity of the Sirbonian Sea, the coastal lake we have already described. When Titus marched from Tanis to Heracleopolis and Pelusium, he came next to the temple of Casian Zeus (Zeus Kasios) which must, therefore, have been near the Sirbonian Sea. Herodotus (II, 6; III, 5) mentions a "Casian mountain" by the Sirbonian Sea. Some think the temple of Casian Zeus was on this "mountain" and is represented by ruins excavated by J. Clédat at a place now called Mahammadiyeh at the west end of the Sirbonian Sea.[9] Others think the temple was twenty-five miles farther along the way and out at a broad place on the narrow spit of land between the lake and the Mediterranean, known as Ras Qasrun.[10] The Casian Zeus (Zeus Kasios) may have been the same as the Semitic god, Baal Zaphon, whose main sanctuary was on the Casian mountain (Mons Casius) up in Phoenicia. If all of that is correct, then the place called Baal-zephon in Exodus 14:2 could have been here near the Sirbonian Sea. If the Israelites did come this way, although the main road ran on the inland side of the lake, they might have gone around on the narrow spit of land between the lake and the Mediterranean, and that could be where the sea a little later washed over and engulfed the pursuing Egyptians. In that case, Eissfeldt suggests, the Israelites may first of all have thanked the god, Baal Zaphon, for their deliverance.[11]

Even apart from Eissfeldt's final conclusion that Israel believed it owed its rescue to Baal Zaphon, which goes contrary to every indication in the Old Testament, there is much to make us doubt the correctness of the foregoing theory. The identification of Zeus Kasios with Baal Zaphon may be correct, and there may have been a sanctuary of this deity near the Sirbonian Sea, but that was not the only sanctuary of this deity in Egypt. Clédat found not only the already mentioned temple of this god at Mahammadiyeh near the Sirbonian Sea, but also another of the same deity at Tell Farama, ancient Pelusium. Also a Phoenician papyrus mentions Baal Zaphon as one of the gods of Tahpanhes.[12] Also Papyrus Sallier IV mentions the same deity as among the gods of Memphis.[13] Therefore, the name of the god as the name of a place could occur elsewhere in Egypt. Furthermore, if the Israelites did go by the Sirbonian Sea they would have had to go on by the way of the land of the Philistines, and historical probability as well as the biblical text (Exodus 13:17) alike speak against that, as we have already argued.

The second way, in general, to go from Egypt to Palestine by land was out across the peninsula of Sinai. This was the wilderness route. In addition to the first strip of fertile land, described above, which runs northeastward from the delta to give access to the coast route to Palestine, there is a second strip of fertile land which runs eastward from the delta to a point about on the middle of the present Suez Canal. This corresponds with the Wadi Tumilat which was described in our first chapter. The ancient Pharaonic canal ran through this valley; the modern railroad goes through it too. In all times it has provided a route of entrance and departure. At the eastern end of the wadi is Lake Timsah, or Crocodile Lake, and beyond that is the wilderness. At Ismailia on the lake, the railroad turns and runs forty miles north to Port Said on the Mediterranean, or forty-five miles south to Suez on the Red Sea. The Suez Canal itself comes right through Lake Timsah and goes on southward to run through the Bitter Lakes and on to the Gulf of Suez. As for the ancient canal which came through Wadi Tumilat, instead of running into Lake Timsah it turned and ran south a few miles farther to connect with the Bitter Lakes.

Since there is no evidence of any route around the north end of Lake Timsah,[14] the usual way to get on out into the wilderness must have been around the south end of this lake or, in other words, between the south end of this lake and the north end of the upper and large Bitter Lake. The strip of land in question between Lake Timsah and the large Bitter Lake is perhaps six miles in length. Here, a little south of the middle of the strip, there is a place known as Serapeum. In 1929, in work of enlargement of the Suez Canal, the ruins of an ancient monument were found here. The remains carried the cartouche of Ramses II and an inscription saying, "The king fortifies the mouth of the canal of Theku."[15] Here then, guarding the last stretch of the canal just to the west, and facing in the other direction eastward toward the great wilderness, the Egyptians evidently had another of their border fortresses. In the northeast, the border fortress of Thel marked the beginning of the coast route; here this fortress marked the beginning of wilderness routes out across the peninsula of Sinai. Bearing somewhat to the left, one could go toward Beersheba; bearing somewhat to the right, one could go toward Aqabah.[16] The route coming from the direction of Beer-sheba is probably what is mentioned in Genesis 16:7, where it is called "the way to Shur." Indeed, according to Exodus 15:22, the whole vast wilderness east of the Egyptian border was called "the wilderness of Shur." Since Shur means "wall," the reference of the name is probably to the line of Egyptian fortifications along that border. So the major way to go from the delta out into the great peninsula of Sinai was to go east through the Wadi Tumilat and out past the border fortress between the Crocodile Lake and the Bitter Lake into the wilderness of Shur. This was the way to start on the wilderness route to Palestine.

Even as Exodus 13:17 refers to the first or coast route and says four things about it, so Exodus 13:18 refers to the second or wilderness route and provides four corresponding or contrasting points of information about it. The passage reads: "But God led the people round by the way of the wilderness toward the Red Sea." The points of information are: (1) As to name, the route is called "the way of the wilderness," a designation which certainly fits the way to which we have just pointed. The only problem lies in the fact that the words Red Sea (or Reed Sea, an interpretation which will be discussed later) are added immediately afterward. In Hebrew the words are *yam suph*, and they are added to the mention of "the way of the wilderness" without any connecting word: *derek ha-midbar yam suph*. They must be intended to specify something particular about the wilderness way which was taken, for after all, as we have seen, it was possible to turn out in different directions across the great wilderness. Perhaps it would be best to translate the whole phrase, "by the way of the wilderness by the Red Sea," with which we may compare Deuteronomy 1:40, "take your journey into the wilderness by the way of the Red sea" (KJV). This must mean, therefore, that the particular wilderness way which the Israelites took, led down by the Red Sea. (2) As to relative convenience, this was obviously a less direct route to Palestine than the coast route. Hence it is said that they went "round" (RSV) or "about" (KJV). This was a more roundabout way. It was farther and more difficult to get across to the beginning of it; it was farther and harder all the way. (3) In character, the wilderness route was less regularly used by military expeditions, hence on this way the people could hope for less molestation and for greater freedom. Also, out here somewhere in this vast wilderness Moses had met God and been sent back by him to his work in Egypt; perhaps it might be hoped that out here the people, too, might be brought more closely into relation to the Lord. (4) As to usage of this route by the Israelites, God led them this way.

Now it is necessary to look at the several stages and stopping points on the way, which are recorded, and see if they indeed fit in (as far as we can tell) with a journey in this general direction into the wilderness. The first stage is given in Exodus 12:37: "And the people of Israel journeyed from Rameses to Succoth." In our first and second chapters we established as probable in our view the facts that the land of Goshen, in which the children of Israel settled in Egypt, was equivalent to the Wadi Tumilat; and that the cities of Pithom and Raamses, in the construction of which they were enslaved, were at Tell er-Retabeh in the middle of Wadi Tumilat, and at San el-Hagar (and nearby Qantir) some thirty miles north and a little west of Tell er-Retabeh. When it came time for the exodus, therefore, many of the Israelites were up at Raamses, where they worked as slaves and where Moses confronted Pharaoh on their behalf; and many were down in Wadi Tumilat, where they also worked at Pithom, and where their homes were in the land of Goshen. The place where the negotiations with Pharaoh were conducted and the final decision made, and the farthest point from which the march began, was Raamses. This is exactly what Exodus 12:37 states: "And the people of Israel journeyed from Rameses." From there they went "to Succoth." In our first chapter we saw that the Egyptian name for the eastern half of Wadi Tumilat was Tjeku or Theku, and we have also noted just above an inscription of Ramses II at Serapeum which speaks of "the mouth of the canal of Theku." As we also observed in the first chapter, unlikely as it may seem at first sight, Theku can very well be transcribed in Hebrew as Succoth, since the Egyptian $\underline{t}$ regularly becomes the Hebrew *s*. Accordingly, in the first stage of the journey, Moses and the Israelites who had been at Raamses came down to Theku or Succoth, that is, to the Wadi Tumilat, to get the others, and it was from there that they all moved on together.

The second stage is given in Exodus 13:20: "And they moved on from Succoth, and encamped at Etham, on the edge of the wilderness." From Numbers 33:8 we may gather that the wilderness of Shur (Exodus 15:22) was also called the wilderness of Etham, and that name was presumably derived from this place of Etham which was "on the edge of the wilderness." The name Etham is probably the same as the Egyptian word $\underline{h}$ t m or *hetem*.[17] This word means "fort." It is used for the fortress of Thel, where the coast route began. It is also used in the report of the frontier official who wrote (as quoted in our first chapter) in the late Nineteenth Dynasty, at the end of the thirteenth century, about letting the Bedouin tribes go past "the Fortress [of] Merneptah . . . which is (in) Tjeku" on their way to the pools of Per-Atum (= Pithom). Since Tjeku was the eastern portion of Wadi Tumilat, that fortress must have been the one which commanded the eastern entrance to Wadi Tumilat; therefore, it was the one between Crocodile Lake and Bitter Lake where we found the ruins of building work by Ramses II; now, somewhat later, it is called the fortress of the next Pharaoh, namely, Merneptah. It is probably this fortress or *hetem* which is called in Hebrew, Etham. The second stage of the journey, therefore, was for the whole people to move eastward through the Wadi Tumilat, the very way their ancestors had come in many years before, to the edge of the wilderness and the beginning of the wilderness route at the frontier fortress between the two lakes. Here, we assume, the people thought they were about to start on the wilderness road before them, but here a surprising change in plans took place.

The third stage of the journey is described in Exodus 14:2: "Tell the people of Israel to turn back and encamp in front of Pi-ha-hiroth, between Migdol and the sea, in front of Baal-zephon; you shall encamp over against it, by the sea." This is stated in such a way that it could be taken as just an arbitrary command of the Lord. On the theory, however, that he actually worked through the things that transpired, and turned even apparent evil into actual good, we may suppose that at the frontier fortress the commanding officer was unwilling to believe that Pharaoh was really letting these people go, and either refused them permission to pass at all, or at any rate proposed to hold them up indefinitely. In terms of the verb employed, to "turn back" means to make a change of direction and a change which involves a setback.[18] Moving previously from west to east toward the border and the wilderness, the people must now have pulled back somewhat toward the west. This was the surprising change of plans that was forced upon them. Would they retreat and turn north? No, that would be back toward the centers of Egyptian power and at best toward the coast route which there was every reason not to take. Would they pull back to the west and then turn to the south? Yes, that would mean a southwesterly course around the bulging upper part of the large Bitter Lake.[19] Then where? The mountain range, Jebel Jenefeh, comes in from the west, and that forces them to move southeastward, between the mountain on the one hand, and the Bitter Lakes, the large one and the small one, on the other hand. At this point they are moving toward what is today the south end of the small Bitter Lake, where the Suez Canal comes from the lake and runs on ten or twelve miles to the Gulf of Suez.

What was the situation at that time at the south end of the small Bitter Lake? In the first place, the Bitter Lakes were probably then connected by water with the Gulf of Suez. Surely the only reason that the Pharaonic canal (which was undoubtedly older than the time with which we are dealing) came through the Wadi Tumilat and turned down to the Bitter Lakes, was that water connections existed on to the Gulf of Suez and the Red Sea. In fact, an extensive study of the area was made by C. Bourdon, a marine official connected for many years with the Suez Canal. He ascertained that the ancient levels of the Bitter Lakes and of the Gulf of Suez were not much different, and that marine shells were to be found all along the banks of the entire depression of Suez and the Bitter Lakes. He concluded that at the time of Ramses II and long afterward the Bitter Lakes were connected with the Gulf of Suez by shallow channels, and that the tides from the Gulf swept all the way up to the Lakes.[20]

In the second place, as just stated, these waters which connected the Bitter Lakes and the Gulf of Suez were relatively shallow. On a detailed map of the southern part of the small Bitter Lake it is possible to see ancient ruins and tracks on either side of a specially narrow and shallow place, and this might well have been passable as a ford under favorable conditions of tide and wind, and impassable under unfavorable conditions.[21] The fact that the ford is no longer usable at all is due to the raising of the level of the Bitter Lakes by the digging of the Suez Canal.[22]

It may also be noted that on a height known as Jebel Abu Hasan, which overlooks this ford from the west, there are the ruins of a square tower discovered by Clédat. This tower was built of large blocks of stone; the interior was divided into three chambers, of which the innermost was a shrine; there were carvings and hieroglyphic texts, chiefly in the shrine room, which contained the names of Seti I and Ramses II.[23] Such an Egyptian tower was known as a *m k t l*, which is the same as the Hebrew word Migdol.[24] An Egyptian papyrus mentions a Migdol of Seti I near Succoth, which could have been this very one.[25] There were of course other Migdols in Egypt, and Jeremiah (44:1; 46:14) and Ezekiel (29:10; 30:6) mention one which was up in the northeastern corner of the land. The one just described, however, can very well be the one mentioned in Exodus 14:2. As to the other two places mentioned in the same verse, Pi-ha-hiroth and Baal-zephon, there are possible suggestions as to their location in this same area but as yet no positive identification.[26]

Between Jebel Abu Hasan and the small Bitter Lake there is a plain perhaps five miles across, and this can be where Israel encamped "between Migdol and the sea" (Exodus 14:2). Behind them was the mountain with the Egyptian watchtower on it; before them was what is now the lower part of the smaller Bitter Lake but what was then a continuous sheet of water extending all the way to the Gulf of Suez. At a shallow point and under very favorable circumstances of tide and wind, that water was probably crossable; under other conditions and particularly for a multitude on foot, it was an impassable barrier. When the people were hemmed in here between the mountain and the sea, Pharaoh could describe their predicament accurately in the words: "They are entangled in the land; the wilderness has shut them in" (Exodus 14:3). Having changed his mind about letting them go, he could pursue them with every expectation of capture.

We have now traced the path of the Israelites, according to our reconstruction, to the point of their involvement in this predicament, and we turn next to the parting of the sea. In Exodus 14:2 the water in front of the Israelites is called the "sea" (Hebrew, *yam*), as it is also in other passages. In Exodus 13:18, as already noted, and also elsewhere (Exodus 15:4, etc.), the water is called *yam suph*. As noted above in our second chapter, the Hebrew word *suph* is the same as the Egyptian *ṯ w f*, which occurs in Papyrus Anastasi III where it is translated "reed-thicket" or "reed-swamps" and where it describes the papyrus marshes in the vicinity of Per-Ramses.[27] It is also used in Exodus 2:3, 5 for the reeds in the Nile. Therefore, the best translation of *yam suph* is evidently "Sea of Reeds," and this rendering is given by Moffatt. In the Septuagint, however, the name was translated as "Red Sea," and this is the rendering which is followed in most English versions. In I Kings 9:26 the name *yam suph* is plainly applied to the Gulf of Aqabah, and this is perhaps the reference in some other passages too.[28] Therefore, we must conclude that this name, Sea of Reeds, and later Red Sea, was applied to the whole of what we know as the Red Sea, including its two gulfs, the Gulf of Aqabah and the Gulf of Suez. As we have seen, the Gulf of Suez extended at this time all the way up to the Bitter Lakes where the Israelites were.

The parting of the water for the crossing of the Israelites is said in Exodus 14:21 to have been accomplished when the sea was driven back "by a strong east wind all night." It would seem unlikely that a straight east wind would have this result at this point, but the Hebrew text of the Old Testament does not give intermediate directions such as northeast or southeast, and the situation would make it seem likely that a strong northeast wind, combined with a strong outgoing tide, could have produced the remarkable "dry ground" on which the Israelites crossed. Likewise the cessation or turn of the wind, along with the incoming of a strong tide, could have produced the flooding of the same crossing in which the Egyptians were engulfed. By way of comparison, it is reported that in the spring the high winds off the Persian Gulf, coupled with high tides, blow in waters to cover an area extending inland for twenty-five miles.[29]

One other point may be noted, namely, that it was the Egyptians, specifically "the chariots and the horsemen and all the host of Pharaoh" (Exodus 14:28), who perished in the sea. Although it is said in Exodus 14:8, 10 that Pharaoh pursued the Israelites, the text nowhere states that Pharaoh himself lost his life in the waters. If he did come all the way in person, he may well have been commanding from the rear; the statement that Pharaoh pursued could even mean only that the government did this. By our reckoning, the Pharaoh involved was Ramses II, and his mummy, already mentioned in our second chapter, is preserved in the Cairo Museum.[30]

We have endeavored to discern what we can of the external circumstances of the great event of deliverance in which the children of Israel were enabled to escape from the land of their bondage. We turn now to the perception of the meaning of the event. Both in the song of Miriam in Exodus 15:21 which many of even the most critical scholars agree was actually sung at that time—

> Sing to the Lord, for he has triumphed gloriously;
> the horse and his rider he has thrown into the sea

—and in the song of Moses and the people of Israel in Exodus 15:1-18 which may have been completed later, since it seems to reflect the further journey, this wonderful deliverance is attributed to the Lord and he is thanked for it. It may seem that in our own foregoing exposition of the biblical narrative we have explained the event as taking place through a remarkable but natural occurrence. This is, in fact, the way in which the text itself states that the wonder was wrought, for it speaks explicitly of the strong east wind which blew the waters back. The event was on that account, however, no less wonderful and no less something for which to thank God. Unexpected and beyond their own power to accomplish as it was, the event was experienced by the children of Israel, perhaps in the light of prophetic interpretation by Moses, as a miracle.

In his discussion of this miracle, Martin Buber defines "miracles" as involving two things in the mind of the one who experiences it. The first is an "abiding astonishment." The person of religious understanding abides in that wonder, and no causal explanation can weaken the wonder.

The great turning-points in religious history are based on the fact that again and ever again an individual and a group attached to him wonder and keep on wondering; at a natural phenomenon, at a historical event, or at both together; always at something which intervenes fatefully in the life of this individual and this group.

The second thing is a transparency of the cause-and-effect sequence through which it is seen that the only real power at work is that of God.

The real miracle means that in the astonishing experience of the event the current system of cause and effect becomes, as it were, transparent and permits a glimpse of the sphere in which a sole power, not restricted by any other, is at work. To live with the miracle means to recognize this power on every given occasion as the effecting one. That is the religion of Moses . . . and that is religion generally, as far as it is reality.[31]

It was in this way that the great deliverance of Israel at the sea was the redemptive event with which their very existence as the people of God began. From the day of this event on, there has persisted in biblical religion a sense of abiding wonder at what the Lord has done, and is therefore always able to do, namely, to redeem his people.

# 7 FROM EGYPT TO SINAI
## (Exodus 15:22-17:16)

After making their escape from Egypt, the Israelites moved out across the peninsula of Sinai. As we endeavor to follow the journey of Israel, it will be of interest to inquire about the people who went. In the usual translations of the texts, Exodus 12:37 tells us that there were at the start of the journey about 600,000 men on foot, besides women and children; Numbers 1:46 reports an actual census in the second year, at Sinai, in which every man able to go to war was counted, to the total of 603,550; and Numbers 26:51 tells of a count of the second generation, when these reached the plains of Moab by the Jordan, with a total of 601,730. If the number of men was some 600,000, the total number, including women and children, must have been at least two or three times as great; therefore, a grand total of one or two million people is indicated.

An approximate idea of the probable total population of Egypt at that time can be gained from the fact that, in the middle of the first century B.C., Diodorus (I, 31, 8) says it was then about seven million, and states that it was "of old" about the same. Similarly, in the first century A.D., Josephus states that it was then seven million five hundred thousand.[1] As for the land of Goshen, we saw in our first chapter that this was probably equivalent to the Wadi Tumilat, and that this area has supported from four thousand Bedouins to twelve thousand agriculturalists. Likewise the Sinai peninsula now supports in its oases some five thousand Bedouins.[2] As compared, then, with the estimates we are able to make of the total population of Egypt at the time, and of the numbers whose subsistence could be provided in the land of Goshen and in the

90

peninsula of Sinai, a total number of one or two million Israelites seems disproportionately high.

Two general lines of approach have been taken in the attempt to ameliorate the difficulty. One approach purports to explain the origin of the figures, but at the same time makes them purely imaginary. The characters of the Hebrew alphabet are used not only for letters but also for numbers. The first character, Aleph, has the numerical value of one; the second, Beth, the value of two; and so on. If we write "children of Israel" in Hebrew and set down the numerical values of the several characters, we find that they total 603. Multiplied by 1000, we would have the 603,000 of the census of Numbers 1:46.[3] But we would not thereby explain the other figures in Exodus 12:37 and Numbers 26:51, nor would we explain the more detailed figures which are stated in hundreds and tens, such as 550 and 730.

The other approach finds the difficulty in our own understanding of the Hebrew text. In the Hebrew text it is actually stated, in Exodus 12:37, that the number of men at the start was "about six hundred *'elef*," and the same word *'elef* appears similarly in the other numerical listings. This word is indeed used in Hebrew as a numeral and as such it means a "thousand." For example, in Numbers 35:4 the pasture lands of the Levites are said to reach outward from the city wall a thousand (*'elef*) cubits. But the word is also used as a noun. As a noun it may mean a "thousand," that is a company of a thousand men, united under one superior or leader. A company of a thousand men was a unit in military organization. An example of the usage of our word with this meaning is probably to be seen in I Samuel 29:2 which, describing a review of the Philistine army, says in the Revised Standard Version: "The lords of the Philistines were passing on by hundreds and by thousands." But even if the *'elef* was in later times a military unit of a thousand men, and if from this usage the word *'elef* came to be used not only as a noun but also as a numeral, namely, the number one thousand, it could still be true that in earlier times the *'elef* was a unit of smaller proportions.

In Judges 6:15 Gideon, making excuse that he cannot deliver Israel, says:

> Behold, my *'elef* is the weakest in Manasseh,
> and I am the least in my family.

In this passage the King James Version translates *'elef* as "family," making Gideon say that his family is poor in Manasseh, and that he himself is the least in his "father's house." Thus he refers to his family twice, once in its relation to the whole tribe, and once in his own relation to it. The Revised Standard Version, however, translates *'elef* as "clan" and thereby Gideon refers, in an even more impressive balance of clauses and progressive restriction of focus, to the relative insignificance of his clan in his tribe, and of himself in his family. Therefore, the word *'elef* must have once been the designation for a unit within a tribe, possibly a "family," more probably what we might call a "clan"; from that earlier usage it came later to designate a standard military unit of a thousand men, and to serve as the numeral one thousand.

We return, then, to the figures which give the number of the Israelites, and take Numbers 1:21, for example. Here the figures for the tribe of Reuben are forty-six *'elef,* and five hundred. The King James Version translates: "forty and six thousand and five hundred"; the Revised Standard Version: "forty-six thousand five hundred." We will now understand, however, that the former part of this listing does not mean forty-six thousand but, rather, forty-six units within the tribe, either "families" or "clans." As for the latter part of the listing, in this case the figure five hundred, this may then be taken as the number of persons in the forty-six families, or the number of men of military capability in the forty-six clans. Transcribing what is given in Numbers 1, in accordance with this understanding, we have the following tabulation:

| Tribe | Units | Numbers |
|-------|-------|---------|
| Reuben | 46 | 500 |
| Simeon | 59 | 300 |
| Gad | 45 | 650 |
| Judah | 74 | 600 |
| Issachar | 54 | 400 |
| Zebulun | 57 | 400 |
| Ephraim | 40 | 500 |
| Manasseh | 32 | 200 |
| Benjamin | 35 | 400 |
| Dan | 62 | 700 |
| Asher | 41 | 500 |
| Naphtali | 53 | 400 |
| Total | 598 | 5550 |

Comparison between the "units" and the "numbers" gives an average of 9.3 persons per unit. W. M. Flinders Petrie, who first pursued this line of explanation of the word *'elef,* considered the units to be "tent groups" and supposed that the average one was made up of two grandparents, two parents, three children, and two herdsmen or hangers-on out of the "mixed multitude" (Exodus 12:38) who went with Israel, which would agree well with the average figure of nine persons per group.[4] George E. Mendenhall, who follows the same general line of explanation but dates the lists (Numbers 1 and 26) shortly after Gideon, perhaps in the twelfth century B.C., thinks the units are tribal "subsections" and the numbers are the numbers of men subject to military service.[5] For ourselves, we adopt the explanation of *'elef* as meaning a unit within a tribe, possibly a family, probably a clan, and we leave the census lists of Numbers 1 and 26 where the biblical text places them, as relating to Israel in the wilderness. The total of the units, which is five hundred and ninety-eight in Numbers 1 and five hundred and ninety-six in Numbers 26, agrees well with Exodus 12:37 which we interpret as meaning that there were, in round numbers, six hundred units upon the departure from Egypt. The total of the numbers, which is 5550 in Numbers 1 and 5750 in Numbers 26, will no doubt have to be taken as the number of men capable of war, since the enumeration was of all who were "able to go forth to war" (Numbers 1:20, etc.; 26:2), and since Exodus 12:37 also makes separate mention of the women and children. Even so, multiplying the number of men by two or three to get the probable grand total of the people, gives a result not too far out of line with what we have seen were the historical probabilities, and a result certainly closer thereto than the supposition, based upon misunderstanding of the word *'elef,* that the number ran into the hundreds of thousands and millions.

Next, we endeavor to visualize the procession of the people as they marched. Exodus 13:18 states that the people of Israel went up out of the land of Egypt "harnessed" (KJV) or "equipped for battle" (RSV). The Hebrew word which is in question here (*hamushīm*) is not very well known. In Joshua 1:14 the word can well mean "armed" (RSV); and some think it can be connected with an Egyptian word meaning "armed with a spear." Undoubtedly, the Israelites were armed; in the wilderness they were soon involved in battle with the nomadic Amalekites (Exodus 17:8 ff.). There is, however, another possibility as to the meaning of the word. The Hebrew *ḥāmēsh* means "five" and *ḥamushīm* could be the plural, meaning "by fives"; similarly, the Arabic *ḥamis* means "in five divisions." Hence the text could state that Israel went up out of Egypt "in marching order." Perhaps we are to think of a main body, preceded by an advance guard, followed by a rear guard, and flanked by guards on either side.[6]

Numbers 2 gives more details as to the arrangement of the camp and the order of march as adopted at Sinai. In the camp the "tent of meeting," which they now had, was put in the middle, together with the Levites who cared for it. Around them in a square were the other twelve tribes (counting the two sons of Joseph, Ephraim and Manasseh, as separate tribes made a total of twelve tribes even without Levi). On the east were Judah, Issachar, and Zebulun; on the south, Reuben, Simeon, and Gad; on the west, Ephraim, Manasseh, and Benjamin; on the north, Dan, Asher, and Naphtali. On the march the tribes moved out from their places in the encampment in orderly fashion, first the eastern three tribes, next the southern three, then the Levites with the tent of meeting, after that the western three tribes, and finally the northern three. Thus here, too, there is a fivefold arrangement.

Also according to Numbers 2, each group camped and marched under its own standard or ensign. Later, the Jewish rabbis worked out a list of these standards, deriving their designs from biblical clues such as what Jacob said about his sons in the blessing in Genesis 49, and other references. For example, the flag of Judah was sky blue with the figure of a lion, since Jacob had said that Judah was like a lion (Genesis 49:9); and the ensign of Issachar was black with sun and moon upon it, since, according to I Chronicles 12:32, the men of Issachar had "understanding of the times," that is, were astronomers and experts on the calendar.[7] The use of standards is, at all events, not unlikely. Already in prehistoric Egypt, boats bear standards; in hieroglyphic, similar ensigns mark local communities; and in connection with warfare, standards are frequently mentioned in Egyptian inscriptions and shown in carvings.[8]

It is further stated in Exodus 13:19 that Moses took the bones of Joseph with him. According to Genesis 50:25-26, Joseph made the sons of Israel promise that, when they finally left Egypt, they would carry his remains with them; upon his decease, he was embalmed and put in a coffin in Egypt. Now we must envision the remains of Joseph carried faithfully on the long march. Thus the bones of the lad who had come so long before to servitude in Egypt were now carried back to his homeland in honor. Finally, burial was made at Shechem (Joshua 24:32).

We also learn from Exodus 13:21 that there went ahead of the people, by day, a pillar of cloud and, by night, a pillar of fire. There are references by ancient historians and later travelers to the practice of Persian armies and Arab caravans of carrying at the head of their line of march braziers of burning wood. It is also recorded that Alexander the Great found the trumpet signal insufficient, hence carried upon a high pole a fire which gave a signal of fire at night and of smoke in the daytime.[9] Something of this sort, it seems probable, is what Israel did too. Since it was, in deepest truth, their God who was leading them, they came to speak of the fire and the smoke as the mark of his presence.

Now we may turn to the places to which the Israelites went. According to our view, they crossed the Reed Sea, which then extended that far inland, at the lower end of what is now the Bitter Lakes, and stood then on the edge of the wilderness of Shur, known also as the wilderness of Etham, and thus on the edge of the peninsula of Sinai. Their further itinerary is found in Exodus 15:22 and following, and also in Numbers 33. According to Exodus 15:22-23 and Numbers 33:8, they went three days into the wilderness and came to Marah, which means Bitterness. About fifteen miles down from where they crossed the sea (according to our theory) and on the east side of the Gulf of Suez, the place known as Ayun Musa, or Springs of Moses, is often held to be the site of Marah, but is not actually far enough along the way. Rather, we suppose, they marched at first farther out into the desert for safety, then turned south along the foot of the inland hills which, farther south, would force them out nearer the coast again. A three days' journey on such a route as this should bring them to Wadi 'Amarah, which probably preserves the name of Marah, and to a spring, Ain Hawarah, just south of the wadi.

Elim, which means "trees," was apparently one day's march farther, and was a place of twelve springs and seventy palm trees (Exodus 15:27; Numbers 33:9). Wadi Gharandel, with its pleasant oasis and very good water supply, can correspond with this.

Below here, according to Numbers 33:11, they touched the shore of the sea perhaps at the plain of el-Markhah, where there was an Egyptian quay in the fifteenth century B.C. Here they made preparations, then marched into the wilderness of Sin (Exodus 16:1; Num-

bers 33:11). Arrival was on "the fifteenth day of the second month
after they had departed from the land of Egypt" (Exodus 16:1). In
Egypt the passover lambs were slain on the fourteenth day of the
first month of the year, which was the month Nisan (March/April)
in the later Babylonian calendar evidently used in the reference
in Exodus 12:2 (cf. verse 6 for the fourteenth day), and the departure from the land must have been initiated on the following day,
the fifteenth day of Nisan. In the same calendar the second month
was Iyyar (April/May), the third month was Sivan (May/June),
the fourth month was Tammuz (June/July), and so on. The statement in Exodus 16:1, however, specifies the second month "after
they had departed from the land of Egypt." In terms of the calendar
just outlined, Iyyar was the first month after departure from Egypt,
and Sivan was the second. The arrival at the wilderness of Sin was
accordingly on the fifteenth day of Sivan, that is, about the first
of June. Starting from Egypt on the fifteenth of Nisan and arriving
here on the fifteenth of Sivan, they had been two months on the
way.

The name of the wilderness of Sin may be derived from the
Hebrew *seneh,* meaning "thorn bush." It lies between Elim and
Sinai (Exodus 16:1). If they came in from the sea through the
Wadi Babah to the large plain, Debbet er-Ramleh ("sandy hill"),
they were directly on a line from Elim (Wadi Gharandel) to Mount
Sinai. At Serabit el-Khadem, near here, the Egyptians mined
turquoise in the Eighteenth and again in the Twentieth Dynasties,
but probably not at this time in the Nineteenth Dynasty. The name
of Dophkah, mentioned only in Numbers 33:12 as the next stop,
may be derived from *mafqat,* the Egyptian word for turquoise, and
therefore points also to the vicinity of Serabit el-Khadem. As for
Alush, also mentioned only in Numbers 33:13, it may well be
recognized in Wadi el-'Eshsh some distance southeastward. Rephidim (Exodus 17:1; Numbers 33:14), in turn, may probably be found
in Wadi Refajid at the foot of Jebel Refajid.[10]

Finally (Exodus 19:1; Numbers 33:15), the Israelites reached the
wilderness of Sinai. Here they encamped "before the mountain"
(Exodus 19:2), a mountain which is called both Horeb and Sinai.
The root of the name Horeb may suggest the idea of barrenness and
desolation; Sinai could be a name given to the summit in view of
proximity to the previously mentioned wilderness of Sin.[11] The
itinerary of Israel, as traced thus far, leads to the south central part
of the peninsula of Sinai. Here the large plain, er-Rahah, provides

space and water sufficient for continued encampment. Above the
plain rises the granite range of Sinai. At hand, and presumably the
mountain in question, is Jebel Musa (7519 feet in elevation), with
its highest and northernmost peak now known as Ras es-Sufsafeh.
Nearby is Jebel Katerina, somewhat higher (8551 feet), but with
no suitable place for encampment at the foot. Somewhat farther
away is Jebel Serbal (6759 feet); it has also been thought by some
to be the mountain of Exodus, but this is probably due only to the
fact that it is near Wadi Feiran which was later used as the pilgrim
route for access to this region.[12]

The date of the arrival at Sinai is given in Exodus 19:1. In the
calendar, about which we have already said something above,
the months were determined by observation of the moon, and the
appearance of the new moon marked the beginning of a new month.
Also, the word for "month" was derived (as it is in English too)
from the word for "moon." In Hebrew *yerah* means both "moon"
and "month"; and *hodesh*, which means "the shining, glittering new
moon," is used for the day of the new moon and also for the whole
month. In Exodus 19:1 the word that is used is *hodesh*. This can
mean "month," and the King James Version translates: "In the
third month. . . ." It can also mean the day of the new moon, and the
Revised Standard Version translates: "On the third new moon. . . ."
The second clause of the sentence begins: "the same day . . ." (KJV);
or: "on that day . . ." (RSV). To render as the King James Version
does: "In the third month . . . the same day . . ." leaves the words
"the same day" without any specific reference prior to them to
which they are related; and with this rendering some are con-
strained to think that something has fallen out or been taken out of
the text.[13] But to render as the Revised Standard Version does: "On
the third new moon . . . on that day . . ." obviates the difficulty, for
both phrases refer to a specific day, namely, the new moon day or
the first day of the month.[14] After departure from Egypt on the
fifteenth day of Nisan as we saw above, the first ensuing new moon
was the first day of Iyyar, the second new moon was the first day
of Sivan, and the third new moon was the first day of Tammuz.
Tammuz is equivalent to June/July; the first day of the month
would be approximately the fifteenth day of June. By our reckoning
above, the wilderness of Sin was reached about the first of June; by
the middle of the same month (in our calendar) they had come on
to Mount Sinai.

In Numbers 10:11 departure from Sinai is dated "in the second

year, in the second month, on the twentieth day of the month." The
reckoning is presumably that which is usual in the calendar of
which we have been speaking. The second month is Iyyar (April/
May); the twentieth day of that month is approximately the fifth
day of May. From arrival at Sinai on the first day of the fourth
month of the calendar year, Tammuz (June/July), to departure on
the twentieth day of the second month of the next year, that is Iyyar
(April/May), is approximately ten months and twenty days. For
that long, Israel remained in the wild, stupendous, and awesome
setting of Sinai.

We have dealt with the people and their processional and the
places to which they came; we speak further, now, of their provisions. Water constitutes the first great problem in the desert, especially in the increasing heat of spring and summer, the period
through which the Israelites have been marching in the portion of
their journey just surveyed. Three times the people murmur, made
desperate by thirst. The first time was at Marah (Exodus 15:24).
There was water here, but it was too bitter to drink. Traveling there
in the last century, Georg Ebers found the water of Ain Hawarah
bitterly salty.[15] The water was made palatable when Moses cast into
it a certain tree. Ferdinand de Lesseps, builder of the Suez Canal,
was told by Arab chiefs that they put a bitter thorn into bad water
when they wanted to drink it.[16]

The second time of murmuring, according to the record, was at
Rephidim where there was no water (Exodus 17:1-7). The third
time was later at Kadesh, in the wilderness of Sin, where there was
no water (Numbers 20:2-13). In both of these cases Moses struck
the rock and brought forth water. Exodus 17:7 calls the first place
Massah ("Proof") and Meribah ("Contention"), because there the
people put the Lord to proof. Numbers 20:13 calls the second place
Meribah, because there the people contended with the Lord. In
Deuteronomy 33:8 and Psalm 95:8 Massah and Meribah are also
mentioned together. Therefore, one wonders if perhaps there was
actually just one incident which, in the course of telling about it,
became connected with two different places. If we must choose between Rephidim and Kadesh, the latter seems the more likely. In the
vicinity of Sinai there is mainly granite rock, which is very hard. At
Kadesh there is limestone, which is porous, develops caves, and
collects water. In the latter area, Major C. S. Jarvis tells how a petty
officer accidentally struck water from a limestone rock.[17] Perhaps
from the fact that this incident is mentioned at two different places,

the legend developed which is found in the Targum of Onkelos that the wonderful well of water went with the Israelites on their journeys, a legend to which Paul seems to allude when he speaks in I Corinthians 10:4 of "the supernatural Rock which followed them."

As for food, the other basic necessity for life in the desert, two wonderful happenings helped the Israelites at critical junctures. The first was the coming of the quail (Exodus 16:13; Numbers 11:31-32). According to the account in Numbers, it was a wind which brought the quail in from the sea. The quail is a migratory bird which crosses Sinai in the autumn and the spring. Often, it is said, they arrive from long over-water flight so nearly exhausted that they fly low, or settle on the ground, and are easily caught.[18] In this case, blown by the wind, they arrived in the very vicinity of the Israelite camp.

The discovery of the manna was the second wonderful event (Exodus 16). Dr. F. S. Bodenheimer, late professor of zoology at the Hebrew University, Jerusalem, studied the question of the manna on the peninsula of Sinai and published his results in his book *Insects as Human Food*; his conclusions have recently been cited afresh and evidently fully supported by Marston Bates, zoologist of the University of Michigan, in an article in the *American Scholar*.[19] Many kinds of insects, it seems, live by sucking the sap of plants, and then produce sweet secretions. In Sinai, two kinds of scale-insects live on the tamarisk trees and do this. The secretion is in the form of large transparent drops which dry and fall to the ground; they accumulate particularly during the night when ants do not carry them off. Under chemical analysis the content was found to be mostly a rare sugar; when eaten as a confection it was "delightful." The phenomenon just described occurs in Sinai for some weeks in June-July. It will be remembered that the Israelites arrived at the wilderness of Sin, where the manna was found, on the fifteenth day of the second month after they had departed from Egypt (Exodus 16:1), and that this date corresponds, in our interpretation, to the first of June. That is exactly the time when the remarkable food just described would have become available.

We have now traced the journey of Israel from Egypt to Sinai, noting particularly the people, the procession, the places, and the provisions. It remains only to remark that the journey of Israel is also a picture of the journey of the Christian life. The parallelism is established by Paul when he writes (I Corinthians 10:1-4):

I want you to know, brethren, that our fathers were all under the cloud, and all passed through the sea, and all were baptized into Moses in the cloud and in the sea, and all ate the same supernatural food and all drank the same supernatural drink. For they drank from the supernatural Rock which followed them, and the Rock was Christ.

The journey begins with a great event. For Israel it was the passing through the sea. The cloud was over them, the water before them; but the cloud seemed to protect, and the water parted and they passed through from bondage to liberty. For the Christian the corresponding great event, at the beginning of the way, is baptism. As God performed a great act of deliverance for the Israelites so, too, he does for the Christian, namely, a deliverance from slavery to sin into the freedom of the glorious liberty of the children of God. This is marked by baptism. To mark it rightly, this ought to be a tremendous event, with a symbolism that is mighty and massive in a going down into the water and a passing through it; and with a meaning that is equally great in that, on the other side of the water, there is really a new life.

The journey has a great leader. Paul does not hesitate to say that the Israelites were baptized into Moses, the great leader of the desert way. Christians, clearly, are baptized into Christ, the great leader of our way.

The journey is a time of testing. In the wilderness Israel was in peril and hardship and, often enough, the people murmured and even wanted to turn back. Nor was God well pleased with how they took it, when he had done so much for them. In the world Christians have opposition and adversity. They are the new Israel, and they too must go through their time of testing.

On the journey there is the sustenance of wonderful provisions. Thinking of the manna, Paul can say that the Israelites ate spiritual (KJV) or supernatural (RSV) food; thinking of the water from the Rock, he can say that they drank spiritual or supernatural drink. Their food and drink were material things, but they brought spiritual as well as physical blessing to them. Since that was so, Paul can even say that the Rock, which followed them in the wilderness (using the conception the origin of which we have already explained), was Christ, for he is the one who brings the blessings of the Spirit. Like the manna and the water, he gives us the bread and drink of the Lord's Supper. By this spiritual and supernatural food, we may be sustained on the long journey.

# 8 MOSES AND MONOTHEISM
## (Exodus 18-19)

At this point in our study of the book of Exodus, Moses has led the children of Israel out of Egypt and they are encamped at Mount Sinai. This is an appropriate place for us to stop, too, and try to assess and understand the religious faith which Moses had, and which he was sharing with the people. Whether the religious faith of Moses should be called monotheism has been debated. A widely held view of critical scholarship is that monotheism was the creation of the literary prophets, Amos, Isaiah, and the others, and that there could not have been anything of this sort in the time of Moses, especially not on the part of Moses himself. Thus, for example, in his presentation of *Religion in the Old Testament*, Robert H. Pfeiffer says that there are, for the historian, no doubts about the historicity and genius of Moses and the abiding greatness of his work, but the ascription to him in the Pentateuch of monotheism —as well as of legislation, covenant, and divinely revealed ethical codes—is without justification: it was first Amos who extended the jurisdiction of the Lord beyond Israel and Canaan.[1]

The view which we will present in the following pages is that the Egyptian religion of Moses' time was a paganism which showed remarkable tendencies toward monotheism, yet never broke through its own limits; that a monotheism on the part of Moses was therefore not impossible at that time, yet also not derivable from Egyptian religion by natural evolution; that his monotheism was, in fact, derived from an Israelite heritage and a personal experience; and that the result was nothing less than a religious revolution which gave to all subsequent biblical religion its distinctive character.

We turn first, therefore, to the religious environment of Moses. Defining his position broadly, we may say that Moses lived in the ancient Near East, that is, in the time and area of the great civilizations of Mesopotamia and Egypt. Presumably, he was exposed to the currents of thought of that period and region. Delimiting his place somewhat more narrowly, we remember that he lived in ancient Egypt. According to the biblical record, he was certainly exposed to the intellectual and religious environment immediately about him. In his time, Joseph was married to Asenath, daughter of Potiphera, priest of On (or Heliopolis, as the Greeks called it), a city which (as we noticed already in our second chapter) was a traditional religious capital of Egypt. As for Moses himself, Exodus 2:10 describes him as growing up as the son of Pharaoh's daughter, and Acts 7:22 states that he "was instructed in all the wisdom of the Egyptians." Also Philo, in his *Life of Moses* (I, 23), gives the tradition that Moses was taught by learned Egyptians, and was instructed in arithmetic, geometry, meter, rhythm, harmony, and music, as well as in "the philosophy conveyed in symbols, as displayed in the so-called holy inscriptions and in the regard paid to animals, to which they even pay divine honors." Accordingly, if we seek to understand the religious environment of Moses, we must inquire about the religion of the ancient Near East in general, and of ancient Egypt in particular.

Concerning the general situation in the ancient Near East, it must be remembered that this time and area were far advanced in culture and in speculative thought from prehistoric time and from primitive man, yet that the period was prior to that of Greek philosophy. In a book called *The Intellectual Adventure of Ancient Man* or, in paperback, *Before Philosophy*,[2] several scholars of the Oriental Institute of the University of Chicago have discussed the general outlook of the people of this time and area. The authors point out that there are two chief ways in which it is possible to view things. One is in terms of an "I" and "It" relationship. Here I am the subject and I look at and try to understand an object. In our modern scientific world this is the way we look at almost everything. Often we even look at people in this manner, making them into statistics and specimens. But there is another way of looking at things and even we, with all our science, naturally and necessarily use it often in relation to other living creatures. Here we actually do deal with persons and even with animals in terms of what we may call an "I" and "Thou" relationship. Here life meets life, and we have a direct and emotional knowledge of, and touch with, the other creature.

If modern scientific man looks at the surrounding world as primarily "It," ancient man—as also primitive man—experiences the world around him as "Thou." The beginnings of science existed already in ancient times, since mathematics and astronomy, for example, were already far advanced in both Mesopotamia and Egypt. But at the same time, the powers of nature were personal forces. In Babylonia, the storm clouds were the great bird, Imdugud, which covered the sky with its dark wings. In Egypt, the sky was the falcon, Horus, whose eyes were the sun and moon, and whose breath was the cool wind from the north. In this way, to ancient man all of nature was alive. Since that personal aliveness was certainly something more than man, all of nature was the personal manifestation of the divine. In Mesopotamia, nature was more violent and unpredictable, with torrential rains and raging floods coming at unexpected times. Therefore, the Mesopotamians felt less sure about what the gods were going to do. In Egypt, the land was more protected, and the river was more regular in its flow and annual inundation. Consequently, the Egyptians had a more comfortable feeling of the reliability of the cosmos and the dependability of the gods who ruled it. But both Mesopotamians and Egyptians agreed that nature manifested the divine, and that in the powers of nature man was in the presence of personal divine wills.

Now we will try to outline this ancient religion, including in our purview both Mesopotamia and Egypt as the two main parts of the ancient Near East, but documenting our points chiefly in terms of Egypt as the land where Moses lived.[3] To do this we will also use the customary technical terms for the various points of emphasis.

Ancient religion was polytheism. Since there were many forces in nature, it was readily assumed that there were many different gods. In Mesopotamia, some of the most important forces of nature, and deities in them, were recognized to be: the sky, high over all, known as Anu (the everyday word for sky), representing authority; the storm, violent and powerful in flat, open Mesopotamia, called Enlil, "Lord Storm," standing for force; the earth, fertile and good, sustaining the life of man, recognized as the mother goddess, Ninhursag, the source of life; and the water, found in the sea, rivers, canals, and wells, known as Enki, lord of the earth (since water is an aspect of earth), representing productivity. These and many other deities meet in the assembly of the gods and determine what shall come to pass in the universe.

In Egypt, where the land is virtually without rain, the apparent daily circuit of the sun is the most prominent and important fact. While we may think the sun is too powerful there, the ancient Egyptians rejoiced in the light and warmth it brought. At night, as they said, "the land is in darkness, in the manner of death,"[4] but in the morning the sun rises again and dispels the darkness and the cold. That daily coming up again of the sun was to them the most important of facts. Therefore, the most important god of all was the sun god. He was worshiped specially, from the earliest times, in Lower Egypt at On (Heliopolis); and in Upper Egypt at Edfu, where the great sandstone temple of the sun god is the best preserved of all ancient monuments.[5] In his manifold manifestations the sun god was known by many names. As the star itself, he was Re, and this was his most common name. As the sky falcon with the sun as its gleaming eye, he was Horus. As the youthful sun on the eastern horizon, he was Har-akhte, i.e, Horus-of-the-Horizon. As symbolized in the scarab or beetle, pushing its pellet before it, he was Khepera.[6] As the aging sun on the western horizon, he was Atum. As the shining disk, radiantly visible in the sky, he was Aten. Along with the sun, here were many other heavenly powers. The moon was Thoth and also Khonsu. The heaven was Nut and also Hathor. The air was Shu. The wind was Amon; when he was believed to be one with Re, the god Amon-Re was recognized.

The earth also was a deity in whom the Egyptians recognized Keb, the husband of the heaven goddess Nut. On earth, the great river of Egypt was a prominent feature, and we have already noted, in our third chapter, that the river was worshiped as the god Hapi. Also that important creature of the river, the crocodile, was the god Sobek. Under the earth, where the sun seems to go when it sets, is the land of the dead. On the edge of the western desert, where the sun sinks and where the dead were buried, one saw the jackal slipping by in the shadows of the evening; he became the god of the dead, Anubis. There too, in the underworld, was Osiris. He was worshiped especially at Dedu in the Delta, known later from his name as Busiris; and at Abydos in Middle Egypt, where he was called "the first of those in the West," that is, the king of the dead. Connected with Osiris were Isis his wife, Set his evil brother, and Horus his son.

The several deities we have now named were not all that were worshiped. A small handbook on Egyptian religion enumerates more than eighty. That is polytheism.

Another mark of ancient religion is immanence. The gods were in and somehow behind the forces of nature which they represented. In Egypt Amon-Re combined the powers of the wind and the sun. To him it was said: "Thine is what thou seest as light, what thou passest through as wind." Aten was the very disk of the sun which could be seen in the sky. Many of the gods were manifest in animals, perhaps in an individual creature, more probably in the whole species. It may have been precisely the unchanging species which gave the impression of the superhuman. Even so Keats, in his "Ode to a Nightingale," speaks of how the voice of this immortal bird which he heard at night had also been heard "in ancient days by emperor and clown."⁷

Ancient religion was characterized by idolatry. An idol is an image of a deity. The use of idols means that the gods were represented in tangible, visible ways. Of the sun god there was a remarkable symbol which was carved in the temple at Edfu and which, from there, spread widely. This was a circle, representing the sun disk, with the royal snake and a feathered wing extending outward on either side. Thus, as a winged bird, the sun flies across the sky. Similarly, the figure of a falcon was used for the sun god. But the sun was also carved as a man. As Horus, he was a man with the head of a falcon, surmounted by the sun disk with the royal snake. As Khepera, he was a man with a beetle as a head. As Amon-Re, he was a bearded man with high double plumes on his head.

Thoth, the moon god, was a man with the head of an ibis, or was an ibis itself. Nut, the sky, was a woman bending over the earth. Hathor, the sky goddess, was a woman with the moon on her head; or, being connected with the cow, was a woman with a cow's head, or a woman's face with cow's ears, or the full figure of a cow. Shu, the air, was a man. Hapi, the river, was a man with symbols of fertility. Anubis was a man with the head of a jackal. Osiris was a man, looking like a mummy. Isis was a woman with a character representing her name on her head. Horus was a child on his mother's lap; a child amidst the marsh plants where he was born; a youthful figure on a lotus blossom, pointing his finger toward his mouth; or a man with the head of a falcon.

Mythology characterized ancient religion. Ancient thought was myth-making thought. Experience with the powers in and behind

things was stated in terms of the actions of those powers. Therefore, there were many stories of the doings of the gods. A simple
story about the sun god is represented in many Egyptian carvings.
As on earth the Nile makes it possible for men to travel by boat,
so in the sky there is another Nile and the sun god moves on it in a
boat. He uses one boat in the daytime; at night he moves through
the underworld in another boat; other important gods form his
crew. The representation of a somewhat more complicated story is
carved in the cenotaph of Seti I at Abydos. The sky is the goddess
Nut, and she is bending over the earth, supported by the air, the
god Shu. She has borne the sun, which is a disk at her feet; at the
same time the sun has taken wing as a beetle and soars aloft. But
in the tomb of Seti I at Thebes it is Hathor, the cow, who is the sky
overhead, held up by Shu, the air. A yet longer story which has
more obviously the marks of a narrative is based on this outline:
Osiris was murdered by his brother Set; Isis, his wife, wept until
the Nile overflowed its banks; Osiris was restored to life and went
west to become the ruler in the land of the dead; Horus, his son,
grew up to revenge his murder. As the weeping of Isis shows, this
story has to do with the annual inundation of the Nile.

Ancient religion was also heavily intermingled with magic. Magic
involves secret knowledge and the performance of ceremonies which
are intended to make certain results ensue. Re, the sun god, was
of course very wise. The goddess Isis once caused him to be bitten
by a snake, then promised to heal him if he would tell her his very
most secret name. When she obtained the name in this way, she
was able to use it to do wonderful things. Thoth, the moon god,
was also very wise (especially since the moon was connected with
the calendar) and was the most powerful of magicians. Once when
the child Horus was left alone out in the swamps, he was bitten by
a snake or by a scorpion, and it was Thoth who cured the injury.
Horus, therefore, was also a powerful helper. On one magical stela,
he stands on crocodiles and holds snakes and scorpions in his hands.
If a victim of snake bite or scorpion bite came for help, water was
sprayed on the statue and collected in a pool at its base, and this
water was given to the patient to drink. Such stories and practices
were common in Egyptian magic.

The idea of fate played a prominent role in ancient religion. The
wisdom of the gods was their knowledge of the order of which they
were a part. As in the examples in the preceding paragraph, the
gods themselves have to acquire wisdom and power, and themselves

have to practice magic. Isis made the snake which bit Re by mixing
the spittle of Re with some earth. She cured Re, after getting his
name from him, by sorcery. Thoth brought "great magic" to heal
Horus when he was bitten by the scorpion. This means that the
gods themselves have to call upon and make use of forces outside
themselves. They themselves arise out of something more ultimate
than themselves.

It was, in fact, a widespread ancient idea that there was a
primordial abyss, a primeval ocean, and that everything came out
of it. This idea was especially likely in Egypt. After the annual
inundation, the waters would begin to subside, then the first hillocks
of dirt would appear out of the waters, and on these humps of mud,
newly fertilized by the river silt, plants would begin to grow and
life would appear. So the Egyptians told of a primeval ocean. They
called it Nun, and sometimes they thought of it as itself a god. Out
of this water of chaos, the god who was the creator emerged and
made himself a mound of dry land to stand on. According to the
priests at On (Heliopolis), this god was the sun god, Atum, or Re,
or Re-Atum, and his primeval hill was located within the sun temple
of their city. Priesthoods elsewhere had other ideas about who this
god was and where his original island was. All, however, agreed in
seeing the creator god himself as arising out of something more
ultimate than he. Thus a more mysterious power, which we may
call fate, looms behind the gods themselves.

Thus far we have described ancient religion in general and
Egyptian religion in particular as characterized by the features of
polytheism, immanence, idolatry, mythology, magic, and fate. It is
also to be observed of Egyptian religion that it showed remarkable
tendencies toward monotheism. One example is found in the so-
called Memphite Theology. In the British Museum there is a stone
with a copy of an inscription which may come from the beginning
of united Egypt when the capital was at Memphis, twenty-five miles
south of On. It says that the primeval hill which arose out of the
waters, which could also be thought of as the land of Egypt or as
the whole fruitful earth, was itself the god Ptah, or Ptah-Ta-Tjenen,
"Ptah the Risen Land." It was in his "heart" or mind that Ptah
thought of everything, and with his "tongue" that he commanded
and caused everything to be made. All things are, therefore, manifestations of Ptah. He is also the same as Nun, the primeval ocean;
he is the one who brought into being Atum, otherwise himself wor-

shiped as the creator; and it is he, Ptah, who has created the other
gods, too. At this point the text reads:

He created the local gods, he made the cities, he founded the
provincial divisions. He put the gods in their places of worship. . . .
He made their bodies. . . . And so the gods entered into their bodies
of every kind of wood, of every kind of stone, of every kind of clay,
of every kind of thing which grows upon him, in which they have
taken form.[8]

It is evident that the Memphite Theology was a remarkable attempt to express the unity of the divine, since all things emanate
from Ptah; and to state the idea of creation by the divine word, since
Ptah thinks and speaks in order to have things made. But the
Memphite Theology still allows for the existence of the many gods,
and for their being in their bodies, that is, in statues or idols of
wood, stone, and clay; and it still leaves Ptah himself immanent in
nature, for the material—wood, stone, and clay—of the idols grows
out of him, that is, out of the earth.

The other significant attempt to establish a monotheism in Egypt
was the sun cult of Amenhotep IV. This remarkable king of the
Eighteenth Dynasty, who took the name Akhenaton, "He Who is
Beneficial to Aton," believed that Aton, who was seen in the shining
disk of the sun, was the only god. He called Aton the "sole god,
like whom there is no other." He pictured him as the sun disk with
long rays, each ending in a hand and reaching down beneficently,
bringing light and life. To Aton the king wrote:

How manifold it is, what thou hast made!

Thou settest every man in his place,
Thou suppliest their necessities.

Thou art in my heart.

Notable as this monotheistic movement was, we must also note
restrictions by which it was bound. Even if the king and his family
worshiped Aton alone, the members of the royal court worshiped
Akhenaton himself, for the king was a god in Egypt and this was
not yet denied. As for the god Aton, although not a purely physical
phenomenon, he was yet actually visible in the heavenly body that
arose in the sky.

So even with such remarkable tendencies toward monotheism as
are exhibited in the Memphite Theology and the sun cult of Akhena-

ton, it must be said that Egyptian religious thought did not break free of its essential limits. As Henri Frankfort writes:

The Memphite Theology and the Aten cult may be said to define the limits of Egyptian religious feeling which would brook no interference with two basic truths: that there were many gods and that they were immanent in nature. Only on this basis could the Egyptians combine a profound awareness of the complexity of the phenomenal world with that of a mystic bond uniting man and nature. But to us the immanence of the gods limits their scope; they appear captives of their own spheres of manifestation.[9]

We have now described the religious environment of Moses in Egypt and in the ancient world in terms of a religion which exhibited tendencies, indeed, toward monotheism, but which never broke through its own fundamental limits. We turn next to the religious experience of Moses. In view of what we have seen, it is certainly not impossible that Moses would state a monotheism. He lived, by our reckoning, in the Nineteenth Dynasty and already in the preceding Eighteenth Dynasty Akhenaton had enunciated the thoughts of which we gave a very brief sample just above. Very long before, at the rise of United Egypt, the Memphite Theology was formulated. Moses did not live in prehistoric or primitive time; he lived in ancient time in which, otherwise, tendencies toward monotheism appeared.

But also in view of what we have seen, it does not seem possible to explain any monotheism of Moses as derived from Egyptian religion by a process of natural evolution. In fact, the popular idea of evolution—that there is an automatic development from lower to higher forms—does not seem to apply very well to any creative area of human life. As an example, one may recall the early Egyptian pottery from which W. M. Flinders Petrie developed his "sequence dating" for the predynastic period. Here the first pottery consisted of fine jars with wavy ledges on either side for handholds; but a progressive degeneration of style ensued, until on the sides of the jars there remained only wavy marks used simply as a crude sort of decoration.

As for Egyptian religion, there was certainly no straight line of development in it—such as popular thought supposes to have been exhibited generally in the religious history of the world—from polytheism to monotheism and from idolatry to spirituality. We have seen, for example, that animals had a prominent place in Egyptian religion. Along the line of evolutionary theory just alluded to, we might suppose that the figures of the gods would be found first as fully animal forms, then as human figures with animal heads or other animal traits, and finally as fully human forms. All three forms are, in fact, present but not necessarily in that order. The earliest statues of a god which have been discovered are those of the god Min in human form. The goddess Hathor is represented with a human face and only the horns and ears of a cow in the First Dynasty, but as a cow in late papyri.[10] As for magic, there are spells against serpents in the ancient Pyramid Texts, but it is only concerning the latest period that Adolf Erman says that then the weeds of magic finally overran everything.[11] As for the tendency toward monotheism, of the two examples we were able to cite, that of Akhenaton was shortly prior to Moses by our reckoning, the other was far back in the early period of united Egypt. While it does not seem at all impossible, therefore, for Moses to enunciate a monotheism in his day, it does seem impossible to explain what he did in terms of an inevitable evolution within the Egyptian religion itself. We cannot say that Moses came along at just the right time to "cash in," so to speak, on a natural development which was bound to carry Egyptian religion from polytheism to monotheism anyway. It remains, therefore, to look to the Israelite heritage and the personal experience of Moses himself.

If we ask first about the Israelite heritage of Moses, we remember that when he was born his own parents kept him for the first three months (Exodus 2:2). When he was put in the basket of bulrushes at the river's brink and found by Pharaoh's daughter, his older sister (Josephus says it was Miriam) managed to have his own mother called to care for him. According to Exodus 2:9-10, the mother took the child and nursed him, and he grew, and she brought him to the daughter of Pharaoh. According to Josephus, the mother was permanently entrusted with the nurture of the child.[12] So in his most impressionable, teachable, and formative years Moses was under Israelite influence. Also, even when he was a grown man at Pharaoh's court, it is stated that he went out to "his people" (Exodus 2:11); therefore, he always knew to whom he really belonged.

What kind of religious faith had been preserved among the Israelite people? One might wonder if any of the heritage of their past had survived during the long bondage and amidst the pervasive Egyptian environment; and, in connection with their later making of the golden calf in the wilderness, one may think that the forms of Egyptian religion had in fact become very influential. Nevertheless, it is possible to see that at least some knowledge of the God of the fathers had persisted. In Genesis, we saw that Abraham worshiped God who manifested himself to him, made covenant with him, and went with him. His son, Isaac, and in turn his son, Jacob, knew this God too. He was, accordingly, the God of the fathers. When Moses came back from the desert he was to tell the people that the God of their fathers, the God of Abraham, of Isaac, and of Jacob, had sent him (Exodus 3:15). Therefore, the people must have continued to know this God. Also, Moses called one of his sons Eliezer, a name which combines the words *Eli*, "my God," and *ezer*, "help," and explained the name by saying, "The God of my father was my help" (Exodus 18:4). Therefore, Moses knew God as the God of his very own father. Therefore, Amram his father (Exodus 6:20) knew God, and must have helped his son to know him too.

Also, there was at least some knowledge of God, among the Israelites, under a special name. This name is written in Hebrew with four characters which may be represented in English by YHWH (or JHVH). We supply vowels to go with these consonants and say Jehovah or, probably more correctly, Yahweh, and we translate the name as Lord (RSV). There is also a short form of the name, Yah (Jah), which occurs, for example, in Hallelujah, which means "Praise the Lord." This name, Yahweh, occurs once back in the time of Enosh, grandson of Adam and Eve, where Genesis 4:26 reports: "At that time men began to call upon the name of the Lord." It appears also in the name of Moses' own mother, for Jochebed (Exodus 6:20) means "Yah (=Yahweh) [is] glory." Therefore, Moses knew the Lord God from his Israelite background, and very specially from his own mother and father.

Turning next to the personal experience of Moses himself, we find that there are three times when God is said to have called to Moses from a particular place. These we may consider the three chief points in his personal religious experience. The first is the happening at the burning bush, which was the experience of revelation. When Moses fled from Egypt he went to the land of Midian (Exodus 2:15). Josephus says that a town of this name (Median[e]) was situated by the Red Sea.[13] Ptolemy and Arabic geographers mention a place of similar name east of the Gulf of Aqabah, across from the southern part of the Sinaitic peninsula.[14] According to this evidence, Moses crossed the peninsula of Sinai and went east of the Gulf of Aqabah. There he married Zipporah, daughter of Reuel or Jethro. Later he was pasturing the flock of his father-in-law at the west side of the wilderness, at Horeb (Exodus 3:1). In our preceding chapter we judged Horeb and Sinai to refer to the same mountain; therefore, at this point Moses was back over in the southern part of the Sinaitic peninsula.

There is a theory that Moses learned what he knew about God from Jethro in Midian. The first Midian, from whom the Midianites traced their descent, was a son of Abraham and Keturah, and one of those whom Abraham sent way "eastward to the east country" (Genesis 25:1-6). So the Midianites might have preserved some knowledge of the God of Abraham. But Jethro is described only as the priest of Midian (Exodus 3:1) and not as a priest of the Lord God. Later when Jethro meets Moses and the children of Israel when they have come out of Egypt, he simply learns from Moses what the Lord has done for them, and joins Moses in praising God for it. Similarly other pagans, as Naaman for example (II Kings 5:15), recognized some great deed of the God of Israel without themselves being worshipers of him. What the biblical text actually tells us that Jethro imparted to Moses was not the knowledge of the Lord, but rather some suggestions on judicial procedure, in that he advised him not to try to judge all the people all by himself but to appoint others to assist (Exodus 18).

So, at the time with which we are now concerned, Moses was simply out in the wilderness with the flock. He was not in any area which Jethro had previously designated to him as where the Lord lived. He was not expecting anything in particular to happen. He was just doing his work, out in the vast solitudes, and he was probably still cherishing concern for his brethren in Egypt, intervention on whose behalf had made it necessary originally for him to flee. But then and there it happened, the revelation that marked an absolute beginning.

The revelation took place at the burning bush (Exodus 3:1 ff.). In Hebrew the bush is called *seneh*. In the preceding chapter we saw that this word means "thorn bush" and surmised that, as the characteristic plant of the region, it gave its name both to the wilderness of Sin and to the mountain, Sinai. The event that transpired here is beyond our power or desire to reduce to a natural and understandable happening. It is presumably akin to that which happened to Isaiah when he saw the Lord in the temple (Isaiah 6:1), and to Ezekiel when he heard a voice telling him to stand upon his feet (Ezekiel 2:1). Moses saw the bush burning with fire, yet not burning up, and turned aside to inspect the sight. Then

"God called to him out of the bush" (Exodus 3:4), named his name, and told him to remove his shoes since he was standing on holy ground. Here we are, as Martin Buber writes, in "that singular region where great personal religious experiences are propagated in ways that can no longer be identified."[15]

Like the event, the conversation that ensued is irreducible. There was a commission. Moses is to go to Egypt to bring the people forth. God commands. Moses resists with various excuses, all of which have to fall before the imperative of what God wants him to do. There was also, in the conversation, a communication of what God is. It is not a question of who God is, as if Moses were making a discovery of God for the first time. The identification of the one who calls from the bush is immediately plain. "I am the God of your father," he says to Moses (Exodus 3:6), that is, he is the God of Amram. He is also the God of Abraham, the God of Isaac, and the God of Jacob. Therefore, he is the one whom Moses knows already from his more distant ancestors and from his immediate parents. Moses inquires, however, as to what he is to say if the people of Israel ask concerning the God who has sent him, "What is his name?" (Exodus 3:13). Martin Buber points out that if you wish to ask a person's name in biblical Hebrew, you do *not* ask, "What is your name?" or "What is his name?" *but* "Who are you?" or "Who is he?"[16] Therefore, the question, "*What* is his name?" is an inquiry which asks, What does his name mean? What is his nature? What is his character? So, too, Proverbs 30:4 asks concerning the one who has established all the ends of the earth, "What is his name?" Surely this is not just inquiring after certain syllables, but seeking to know *what* he is.

This is what was communicated at the burning bush. In answer to the question, What is his name? God says to Moses: *Ehyeh asher ehyeh* (Exodus 3:14). Here in the repeated word we have the verb which is connected with the noun Yah or Yahweh, and the verb means "to be." The divine name therefore contains the divine affirmation, "I am," and the simplest translation of the statement is, "I am who I am" (RSV). But what is in view here is hardly an abstract affirmation of pure existence, which is an idea more like what a Greek philosopher might formulate. The same verb has, in fact, just been used also in Exodus 3:12, where God says to Moses, "I will be with you." So to say "I am" carries the concrete idea, "I am present," and "I will be present."[17] This is the mighty assurance which is given to Moses and which, through him, is to be given to the people of Israel. The God who manifested himself to Abraham and went with him, and was similarly known to the succeeding patriarchs, will now also be mightily present with the whole people. He has manifested himself to Moses in the burning bush, and he will manifest himself to them in mighty deeds. He is present with Moses, and he will be present with the people.

The second very important point in the religious experience of Moses, marked by the biblical statement that God called to him from a particular place, is at the time of the "eagle speech" and involves the experience of covenant. Moses is now at Sinai again, and with him are the people whom he has led out of Egypt. "And the Lord called him out of the mountain" (Exodus 19:3). Up on the mountain, God told Moses to tell the people: "You have seen . . . how I bore you on eagles' wings. . . . If you will . . . keep my covenant, you shall be my own possession . . . for all the earth is mine" (Exodus 19:4-5). The great eagle stirs up its nestlings to teach them to fly; it takes a little one upon its own wings until it can launch forth for itself. So the Lord has done with his people. Now he establishes covenant with them, to make them his own "possession" or "peculiar treasure" (KJV). A "peculiar treasure" is a possession upon which one person has a special claim. The covenant made by the Lord with his people is not an agreement between two equals, such as the covenant between Jonathan and David (I Samuel 18:3); but a royal covenant, such as King David made with the northern tribes (II Samuel 5:3), expressive of kingly rule and rightful claim. But let the people not forget that although the Lord has chosen them to be a holy nation, the whole earth is his too; they have no monopoly on him.

The third point at which God called to Moses from a particular place is given in Leviticus 1:1. Moses and the people are still at Sinai. "The Lord called Moses, and spoke to him from the tent of meeting." This again is a specific place, but now it is a portable object that is involved. Let no one think that God resides in a thorn bush or on a mountaintop. He may manifest himself there, but he is not bound to these places. The "tent of meeting," carried with the people wherever they go, will symbolize his meeting with them in any place and every place, for he can be anywhere and everywhere. Here, in the call from the tabernacle, he summons to offerings and sacrifices. These constitute the duties of the people who serve him.

Thus, in the way which we have just outlined, the biblical text indicates these three crucial points in the religious experience of

Moses, the points at which revelation was vouchsafed, covenant made, and duty stated.

We have endeavored to describe the religious environment of Moses; we have sought to understand the religious experience of Moses; we have now to try to grasp the religious revolution of Moses. It is a fact that the religion of the Old Testament is radically different from that of the ancient world otherwise. In *The Intellectual Adventure of Ancient Man*, H. and H. A. Frankfort write: "When we read in Psalm 19 that 'the heavens declare the glory of God; and the firmament sheweth his handiwork,' we hear a voice which mocks the beliefs of Egyptians and Babylonians."[18] To the Mesopotamians the heavens were the highest god Anu; to the Egyptians they represented the divine mother; to the Psalmist they were but a witness to the majesty of God. This idea is found not only in Psalm 19 but in the entire Old Testament from its oldest to its latest parts. Throughout the Old Testament there is a decisive contrast with what we know as ancient religion otherwise. We described that ancient religion above as characterized by belief in many gods who are in nature, who are represented in idols, who are told about in mythology, who are dealt with by magic, and who are themselves subservient to fate. But in the Old Testament there is one God, whose first commandment is to have no other gods before or besides him (Exodus 20:3). This God is above nature, for, having made all things, he cannot be limited within any thing. He is beyond representation, and his second command is to make no graven image (Exodus 20:4). There is no mythology in the sense of fanciful stories about the gods and goddesses in their deeds and misdeeds. There is no magic, for no incantations are used to compel the deity, and no secret knowledge or mysterious practice can exert constraint upon him. There is no fate, no order of necessity above God to which he is subject.

For this religion our best single word is monotheism—the belief in the one God. Over against that as found in the religion of Israel—and in Christianity and Islam which are derived from it—all else is paganism. In contrast with pagan religion, in his book on *The Religion of Israel* Yehezkel Kaufmann, professor of Bible at the Hebrew University, Jerusalem, says that this "biblical religious idea," which he believes is "visible in the earliest strata" of the Old Testament, is the idea of

... a supernal God, above every cosmic law, fate, and compulsion; unborn, unbegetting, knowing no desire, independent of matter and its forces; a God who does not fight other divinities or powers of impurity; who does not sacrifice, divine, prophesy, or practice sorcery; who does not sin and needs no expiation; a God who does not celebrate festivals of his life. An unfettered divine will transcending all being—this is the mark of biblical religion and that which sets it apart from all the religions of the earth.[19]

Since this is the basic idea of Israelite religion it is reasonable to suppose that it came into existence at the same time as the people themselves came into their existence as the people of God, and this, according to their records, was at the time of the exodus and under the leadership of Moses. Moses himself had antecedents, as we saw, in the patriarchs before him. But the clear grasp of monotheism, as we have defined it, and the contrast thereof with paganism, we may believe we owe to Moses. There are no roots in paganism which can explain it.

It is, as Kaufmann says,

. . . a new religious category that is involved, the category of a God above nature, whose will is supreme, who is not subject to compulsion and fate, who is free of the bonds of myth and magic. This idea, which informs all of biblical creativity, is what paganism never knew.[20]

But Israelite religion knows this idea and, from first to last, exhibits it. Therefore, it must have been Moses who grasped it already. He was, accordingly, the initiator of a religious revolution, the creator of an original idea. How can the origin of a new idea be explained? As Kaufmann puts it, "The birth of every original idea is a mystery which defies attempts to account for it."[21] On the human side, we may call the rise of the new idea an intuition. From the divine side, we can call it only a revelation.

# 9 THE TEN COMMANDMENTS
## (Exodus 20-40)

In the preceding chapter we saw that the Israelites probably stayed at Mount Sinai from the first day of the fourth month of the calendar year (about the fifteenth of June) to the twentieth day of the second month of the next year (about the fifth of May), or approximately ten months and twenty days all together. Between Exodus 19:1, which tells of the arrival at Sinai, and Numbers 10:11, which reports the departure therefrom, the biblical text contains mostly laws and some narratives connected with the laws. Among these laws, three main groups are recognizable. As commonly designated, these are: (1) the Ten Commandments (Exodus 20:1-17, with another copy in Deuteronomy 5:1-21, and perhaps a mixed form in Exodus 34:14-26); (2) the Book of the Covenant (Exodus 20:21-23:33); and (3) the Priestly Code (comprising most of the remaining legal material in Exodus and all of it in Leviticus and Numbers).

Where do the laws come from? In their present form, they doubtless come from the priests and scribes of Israel. To pass the laws down through the centuries, the scribes must have copied them over and over. As we know from Ezra (7:6, 10), Jewish scribes were not only copyists but also students and teachers. Therefore, they probably worked on collecting and interpreting the laws too. Also, the priests were much concerned with the laws, especially those concerning worship and sacrifice. Therefore they, too, doubtless worked on formulating and enforcing the laws in the changing circumstances of different times. Indeed it seems to be of the very nature of law that it grows and develops over the years. So we may readily suppose that the whole bulky body of law in Exodus and

Leviticus and Numbers was the result of an extended cumulative development. Even in the case of the Ten Commandments we may note from the references given above that they are preserved in two or three different forms. As to the individual commandments, we observe that some are very short, others much longer. If we suppose that the original form was uniformly concise, we may judge that the longer formulations represent later expansions. The study of this development of the law is important, but it is not our purpose to go into the detail of it here.

In their original nucleus, the laws come from Moses. This affirmation is consonant with the placement of the laws in the Old Testament. The fact that they are collected chiefly within the framework of the period at Mount Sinai points to their derivation, in some manner, from Moses. The supposition to which we are pointing is that the original nucleus of the later vastly expanded code was actually formulated by Moses. This is commonly denied by critical scholarship, as, for example, by Robert H. Pfeiffer in the statement that "objective study shows that none of the Pentateuchal codes could have been promulgated by Moses."[1] Therefore, we must support our supposition by the exploration of several related questions.

Was Moses interested in law? Yes, naturally and necessarily. As we have already seen in our earlier chapters, he had a passionate concern for justice. When first, as a grown man, he revisited his people, he stood up for one of them against an Egyptian taskmaster. When two Hebrews struggled together, he said to the one who did the wrong, "Why do you strike your fellow?" only to be rebuffed: "Who made you . . . a judge over us?" (Exodus 2:13-14). Later, Moses had a pressing burden of judging to carry. A single day in the wilderness is compacted into the statement: "On the morrow Moses sat to judge the people, and the people stood about Moses from morning till evening" (Exodus 18:13). Moses' father-in-law, Jethro, was there at the time. He thought it too much for Moses, and asked why he had to do it. Moses explained: "Because the people come to me to inquire of God; when they have a dispute, they come to me and I decide between a man and his neighbor, and I make them know the statutes of God and his decisions" (Exodus 18:15-16). So Jethro suggested that Moses should still teach the people the statutes, but should also choose trustworthy men to assist and to conduct most of the work of judging.

Was Moses able to read and write? Yes, surely. While it may once have been possible to think of Moses as moving in a primitive environment, we now know, as previously observed in the present book, that his background was the culture lands of the Near East whose history stretched far back before his time. In those lands, writing was probably invented in Mesopotamia around 3500 B.C. and, at the most, not long afterward in Egypt—and that was two thousand years before the time of Moses. Before and by the time of Moses, extensive literatures existed in both Mesopotamia and Egypt. Not only do we have the cuneiform texts of Mesopotamia and the hieroglyphic of Egypt but, on the peninsula of Sinai at Serabit el-Khadem, fifty miles from Mount Sinai, the proto-Sinaitic inscriptions of around 1500 B.C. reveal the existence of an alphabetic script containing most of the letters found in later Hebrew and therefore perfectly suited for the writing of the Hebrew language.[2] In addition to the general situation in the time of Moses, we may recall his own education in particular. According to the references cited already in the preceding chapter, it was an excellent Egyptian education.

Along with this general probability that Moses was a highly literate man, we have specific references in the book of Exodus to his work of writing and reading. At the time of the war with Amalek, earlier in the wilderness, the Lord told Moses: "Write this as a memorial in a book" (Exodus 17:14). At Sinai, after the giving of the covenant code, we have these statements: "And Moses wrote all the words of the Lord" (Exodus 24:4); "Then he took the book of the covenant, and read it in the hearing of the people" (Exodus 24:7). Concerning the Ten Commandments it is said: "And he wrote upon the tables . . . the ten commandments" (Exodus 34:28).

Were there actually written codes of law at that time? Again the answer is yes, and again there are examples from long before Moses as well as after him. In Egypt it is true that no law codes have yet been found. Perhaps, it is surmised, such codes were written on papyrus or leather and did not survive; or, perhaps, the god-king preferred to give his decrees directly.[3] But in Mesopotamia we have: the Sumerian Code of King Ur-Nammu of the city of Ur (c. 2050 B.C.); the Akkadian Code of the kingdom of Eshnunna (perhaps in the first half of the nineteenth century B.C.); the Sumerian Code of King Lipit-Ishtar of Isin (probably around 200 years older than the laws of Hammurabi); and the Akkadian Code of King Hammurabi of Babylon (who probably reigned c. 1728-c. 1686 B.C.). All of these codes antedate Moses by centuries. After him we have: the Assyrian laws (from the twelfth century B.C.);

the Hittite laws (the preserved copy is from around 1200 B.C.; the original must have been substantially older and probably much older than Moses); and the New Babylonian laws (from the time of the New Babylonian kingdom, *c.* 626-539 B.C.).

Were ancient codes of law written in the way in which the Bible pictures the laws of Moses? The account of the war with Amalek and the covenant code are both described as written in a "book" (*sepher*). This word is ordinarily used for a "book" in the form of a scroll. Scrolls of papyrus and of leather are known in Egypt from very early times. Statuettes from early dynasties show scribes writing on rolls of papyrus, while an inscription from the Eighteenth Dynasty makes explicit mention of a roll of leather used for a written record of Thutmose III.⁴ According to Exodus 32:15, 34:28, the Ten Commandments were on two "tables" (KJV; RSV) or "tablets" (Moffatt) of stone. The word for these "tables" (Hebrew, *luhoth;* Greek, *plakes*) means a flat stone. The use of a flat stone for an important inscription is very common in the ancient world. In the form of an upright slab, inscribed or sculptured, we call such a table of stone a "stela" (Greek, *stēlē*). The Code of Hammurabi is preserved on such a stela.

In the light of the foregoing considerations, therefore, there is no difficulty in supposing that Moses could and would and did write down the law of God for his people. But what did he write? That it was the whole Priestly Code we may think was probably not the case. Much of the whole corpus of laws sounds like later time and later practice; as explained above, it can well be the work of later priests and scribes.

That Moses wrote the Book of the Covenant, however, may seem possible. In this code, Exodus 22:5 may be later, since it has to do with agriculture and supposes that the Israelites have their own fields and vineyards, which they did not have in the wilderness. But of the code as a whole, Yehezkel Kaufmann says: "The laws of the Covenant Code are for the most part entirely in accord with the nomadic stage of Israel's prehistory as reflected in the patriarchal narratives. Even such a primitive society has room for laws about slaves, murder, damages, bailees, seduction, and magic."⁵ We may also note that this code has much in common with other early law codes already mentioned. As to form, both in the other ancient Near Eastern codes and in the biblical one, conditional sentences of complex structure are used to describe a case and to define the relevant punishment. "When" or "if" something happens, "and" there is a certain result, "then" such and such a penalty is to be imposed. As to content, note for example a single law which is found both in other codes and in the biblical code. In the Code of Eshnunna (§54) we read:

> If an ox is known to gore habitually and the ward authorities have had the fact made known to its owner, but he does not have his ox dehorned, (and) it gores a man and causes his death, then the owner of the ox shall pay two-thirds of a mina of silver.[6]

In the Code of Hammurabi (§251) the same law is found in this slightly variant form:

> If a man's bull have been wont to gore and they have made known to him his habit of goring, and he have not protected his horns or have not tied him up, and that bull gore the son of a man and bring about his death, he shall pay one-half mina of silver.[7]

In the Covenant Code we find what is very plainly the same law, but with certain not insignificant variations:

> But if the ox has been accustomed to gore in the past, and its owner has been warned but has not kept it in, and it kills a man or a woman, the ox shall be stoned, and its owner also shall be put to death. [Exodus 21:29]

Here the more severe penalty imposed is presumably due to the higher value placed upon human life among the Israelites; noticeable also is the inclusion of the woman as well as the man in the purview of the statute.

This kind of law in general, therefore, and many of these laws in particular, were probably shared by the Israelites with other peoples in the ancient Near East. Since the Code of Hammurabi and the other even earlier Mesopotamian codes are prior to the time of Moses, there is no difficulty about placing Exodus 21:29 and many other laws of the Covenant Code at least as early as Moses. In fact, recent study has suggested that the Code of Hammurabi is more advanced rather than less advanced in comparison with the Covenant Code,[8] and Kaufmann says: "The Covenant Code is to be considered rather an early formulation and crystallization of the common Near Eastern law of which Hammurabi's laws are a more advanced development."[9] In this case, many of these laws might have been known even to the patriarchs when they came from Mesopotamia long before Moses. As they exist in the setting of the Book of the Covenant, where Moses may have written them out, they represent, as Kaufmann also observes, that peculiar mixture and blend of the juridical, the moral, and the religious which we do not find elsewhere and which is characteristically Israelite.[10]

That Moses wrote the Ten Commandments is what we may affirm as most probable. The critical scholarship referred to near the beginning of this chapter, which denies that any of the Pentateuchal codes could have been promulgated by Moses, of course includes in that denial any ascription of the Ten Commandments to Moses. This opinion is not new. Nearly a century ago, when the critical study of the Old Testament was developing, various prominent scholars declared that the Ten Commandments could not be of Mosaic origin but must be much later. Julius Wellhausen[11] thought that Moses dispensed justice orally at the sanctuary for many years, but since there are different traditions, we cannot tell what he really said, and he probably did not write anything down. If there were any stones in the ark at all, there was nothing written on them, otherwise they would not have been kept hidden. The pupils and followers of Wellhausen generally continued along this line. Karl Budde, for example, said that if the Ten Commandments had been given by Moses, "hardly anything could have remained for the prophets to do."[12] Some such opinion is still held by many. The Ten Commandments, they believe, are probably later than the prophets, possibly even as late as or later than the exile, and that means five to seven centuries or more after the time of Moses. Thus Georg Beer, for a single example, holds that the Ten Commandments originated after the people went into exile, that is, after 587 B.C.[13]

But more recently it has been possible to observe at least a growing tendency to think that the Ten Commandments may come from Moses after all. In a study of the Decalogue in the light of more recent research, J. J. Stamm[14] notes that in the period from 1910 to 1930 the majority of scholars still held to the late date of the Ten Commandments, but at least three prominent critical students advanced different views. Hugo Gressmann, in his book on Moses published in 1913 (*Mose und seine Zeit*, pp. 473 ff.), was not sure if the commandments came from Moses himself, but thought that they were at least the "catechism of the Hebrews in Mosaic time." Hans Schmidt, in the Gunkel-Festschrift issued in 1923 (pp. 78-119), argued that Moses gave Israel the Decalogue at Sinai, and that the text was put on two tables of stone which were carried for centuries in the ark. Ludwig Koehler, in an article, "Der Dekalog," printed in a theological review (*Der Theologische Rundschau*) in 1929 (pp.

161-184), suggested that the Ten Commandments were probably an impersonal rather than a Mosaic formulation, but found nothing against their composition in the time of Moses. Continuing the survey into the period since 1930, Professor Stamm finds that the majority of scholars have now come to reckon with the great age if not the actual Mosaic origin of the Decalogue, and that at least several attribute it to Moses himself. The work of three of these scholars will be referred to in what immediately follows, as we set forth our own reasons for thinking that the Ten Commandments were probably written by Moses.

The Ten Commandments are unique. Above, we have already described a type of law which was very widespread in the ancient world. The formulation of the statutes is in terms of cases, and it is stated that "when" or "if" something happens, "and" there is a certain result, "then" such and such is the penalty. This form is found not only in the Code of Eshnunna, the Code of Hammurabi, and elsewhere outside the Bible, but it is also found in the Priestly and the Covenant Codes in the Old Testament. In a study of the origins of Israelite jurisprudence, Albrecht Alt[15] has called attention to the virtual ubiquity of this form of casuistic law in the ancient world outside the Bible, and contrasted with it a different form of law, which he terms apodictic, where the statutes are put in short, positive, declaratory sentences.

This apodictic form is found in a number of places in the Old Testament: in several statements of the death penalty in Exodus 21:12, 15-17; in certain prohibitions in Leviticus 18:7-18; in a series of curses in Deuteronomy 27; and, above all, in the Ten Commandments of Exodus 20 and Deuteronomy 5. While the casuistic laws are shared widely with other peoples of the ancient world, the apodictic laws are peculiar to Israel. The casuistic laws of Israel may have been borrowed from their neighbors; the apodictic laws were their own particular heritage and may have come from their wilderness days. The Ten Commandments were probably recited every year at the feast of tabernacles, which recalled the tents of the wilderness and the time when God delivered the people and made covenant with them. Psalm 81 may have been sung at that feast: it speaks of the deliverance and then moves into the first sentences of the Decalogue. While Alt, in this study, went only so far as to claim that the apodictic laws came from the wilderness days, it does not seem an unreasonable extension of the argument to suppose that at least the Ten Commandments, the most uniquely unconditional laws of all, must have had a unique origin, and to attribute the communication of them to that great and remarkable person, Moses.

The Ten Commandments also fit with the religion of Moses. In his study of the Decalogue, H. H. Rowley traces the Ten Commandments back to Moses. The God of Moses, he observes, was an ethical God. If the religion of Moses had not been distinctive, it would have been swallowed up when the Israelites went in among the Canaanites. That Israel was successful in resistance to Canaanite polytheism must be due to the fact that the Lord whom they worshiped was different from the Canaanite deities not only in numerical uniqueness but also in higher and more consistent ethical character. It is entirely consonant with this fact that the God of Moses was an ethical God, that the Ten Commandments are an ethical Decalogue. Professor Rowley concludes that

. . . an ethical Decalogue is in harmony with the whole character of the bond between Israel and God which Moses mediated. Yahweh had chosen Israel and delivered her from Egypt; Israel in response committed herself in loyalty and obedience to Him. That is the essence of Israel's Covenant with God. It rested on her recognition of what God had done and on her gratitude to Him for His mercy. . . . There was thus an ethical strand in the very establishment of the religion of Israel through Moses, since gratitude is essentially an ethical emotion. . . . It is therefore wholly consonant with the conditions of the time that the fundamental demands of the religion established through Moses should be couched in ethical terms, and far more likely that in such a moment and through such a man this great advance should be made than that it should just happen somehow by itself at some unknown time and in some unknown way.[16]

The Ten Commandments likewise fit with the historical situation of Moses. In his study of Moses from which we have already quoted in other connections, Martin Buber speaks of the Ten Commandments and declares that "each word [is] charged with the dynamism of a historical situation."[17] What was that situation? A group of tribes was becoming a nation. If we take into account the fact that according to Exodus 12:38 a "mixed multitude" went up with the children of Israel, we may say that a conglomeration was becoming a community. The laws we are studying set forth the regulations by which that community is constituted and by which it can exist. Here, in the Ten Commandments, as Buber puts it, are the "fundamentals of community life under the rule of God."[18] Or, to quote Volz, the Ten Commandments are "the Constitution by which the host of Moses became united with their God and likewise among themselves."[19]

So, although in its present form the Old Testament law is admittedly the result of a long development, in its original nucleus and particularly in the form of the Ten Commandments it may be recognized as derived from Moses. But in their ultimate origin we believe that the laws come from God. In the copy which has been preserved, the Code of Hammurabi is carved on a pillar of stone six feet high. In the relief at the top the god Shamash is seated on a throne. He is the sun god, the god of justice and law. Before him stands Hammurabi. The god holds a ring and staff, the insignia of royalty, and extends his hand toward the king to give him the right to promulgate the laws which follow in the cuneiform text of the inscription. Even so, in the narrative of Exodus, God gave Moses the tables of stone on which he had written the law (Exodus 31:18; 32:16) and after the first tables were broken, had Moses write a new set (Exodus 34:28). But on these tables of stone, it may be taken for granted, there were no carved representations of the deity. The commandments they contained forbade not only the worship of other gods but also the making of any graven image. Therefore, the process of the giving of the laws must have been what we would call spiritual. God put his requirements into the mind of Moses to communicate as laws. What was written in the laws was transmitted through the mind of a man, therefore was conditioned by that mind and its environment, yet in the deepest sense was derived from God. Since we believe that what Moses taught about God as the one holy God is true, we may believe that what is written in the Ten Commandments also represents the true requirements of the one God.

As far as the narrative of outwardly spectacular events in the giving of the law is concerned, we may believe that the really significant thing was the thoughts which came into the mind of a man to communicate from his God to his people, and we may picture the happening as Martin Buber does:

If we wish to keep before us a sequence of events possible in our human world, we must renounce all such tremendous scenes. Nothing remains for us except the image, capable of being seen only in the barest outline and shading, of the man who withdraws to the loneliness of God's mountain in order, far from the people and overshadowed by God's cloud, to write God's law for the people. To this end he has hewn stelae out of the stone for himself. It must be stone and not papyrus. For the hard stone is called to testify, to serve as a witness. . . .

And so he writes on the tables what has been introduced to his senses, in order that Israel may come into being. . . . And the tables remain as "tables of testimony" or "tables of making present" (Exodus 32:15), whose function is to make present unto the generations of Israel forever what had once become word; that is, to set it before them as something spoken to them in this very hour.[20]

We have asked and answered the question, Where do the laws come from? and we turn now to the further question, What do the Ten Commandments say? We have already noted that they are concerned with the fundamentals of the life of man in his community, and here we may observe that they state those fundamentals in relation to God, time, and space.[21] We have also remarked already that in their original form all of the commandments may have been expressed very concisely as many of them still are. In quoting them, therefore, we will give only their essential and most compact statements.

The first three have to do with the life of man and his community in relation to God. The first commandment is: "You shall have no other gods before me" (Exodus 20:3). The words translated "before me" (RSV) or "besides me" (RSV margin) are literally "upon my face": the expression supposes other gods set up before the Lord as antagonists and as casting a shadow over his eternal being and true glory.[22] This commandment opposes polytheism and guards the unity of God. The second commandment is: "You shall not make yourself a graven image" (Exodus 20:4). An image is an idol, a visible, tangible object to represent god. This commandment opposes idolatry, and guards the invisibility, immateriality, and spirituality of God. The third commandment is: "You shall not take the name of the Lord your God in vain" (Exodus 20:7). The creature should not speak lightly of the Creator, nor try to use his name for his own purposes. This law opposes blasphemy, perjury, disrespect, and even idle speech and lip service; and it guards the honor of God. Through these three commandments we are taught that God is the only One, the incorruptible Spirit, the glorious Creator. The community can exist aright only if it maintains its existence consciously under him.

The next two commandments may be recognized as having to do

with relationships in time. The fourth commandment says: "Remember the sabbath day, to keep it holy" (Exodus 20:8). The existence of the community and of man is an existence in time. As we move through time we mark our going by natural divisions. The most elementary division is that of the day, demarcated by the rising and setting of the sun. Every seventh day, according to this commandment, is to be sanctified as a day of cessation of work, and as a day of rest. This regulation opposes the dissipation of human energies by unceasing busyness; it guards the natural rhythms of life. The fifth commandment enjoins: "Honor your father and your mother" (Exodus 20:12). The existence of the community and of man in time is an existence which moves not only through the days but also through the generations. Here the successive divisions of time are marked by the generations of parents and children. This commandment opposes the breaking apart of the generations, and guards the continuity of national time. The community and man can move through time aright only if both rhythm and continuity are in the movement.

The last five commandments regulate the relationships of man and his community in space, that is, in the relations of the members of the community with one another. The sixth commandment is: "You shall not kill" (Exodus 20:13). Here is a prohibition of murder. It opposes homicide and probably also suicide, as Augustine held.[23] It guards the sacredness of human life. The seventh commandment is: "You shall not commit adultery" (Exodus 20:14). This opposes sexual immorality, and guards the institution of marriage. The eighth commandment rules: "You shall not steal" (Exodus 20:15). This opposes robbery, whether by violence or fraud, and guards property. The ninth commandment says: "You shall not bear false witness" (Exodus 20:16). This commandment opposes every falsehood, particularly dishonest testimony against another, and it guards the integrity of the word. The tenth commandment reads: "You shall not covet" (Exodus 20:17). This opposes that greedy desire which leads to oppression, cheating, and violence; and it guards the hidden intent, the inward thought. So the community of men can stand firm only if its members guarantee to one another the protection of these things: of life, marriage, property, social honor, and even secret desire.

Finally we ask, What do the Ten Commandments have to do with us? For one thing, they provide a lasting foundation for all community. The life of man is always a life in community and these principles, discerned (or revealed) long ago, appear to be permanently and indispensably relevant to community. In a volume entitled *Foundations for Reconstruction*, Elton Trueblood endeavors to discover the necessary planks for a platform on which civilization must be rebuilt if it is to be rebuilt in enduring fashion, and, taking the Ten Commandments as the framework for the book, he finds in this ancient moral law the indispensable foundation for the present. He writes:

The Ten Commandments constitute the most memorable and succinct extant formulation of the ethical creed of the West. For that reason they provide a convenient statement of the fundamental basis of recovery and reconstruction. What is important, however, is not the particular formulation known as the Decalogue, but the total view of life of which the classic commandments are shorthand representations. Each of the commandments can be greatly expanded; each can be stated in positive rather than negative form and ought to be so stated. When this is done, what we have is not an outworn set of specific prohibitions, but positive principles of such a nature that a good society cannot be constructed or reconstructed without reference to them.[24]

As indispensable foundations for community, the Ten Commandments teach that there can be only one ultimate loyalty. This is the import of the first three commandments. The living God is the only worthy object of such loyalty. It is that loyalty which is the last enemy of every kind of totalitarianism. Concerning the dictators, Walter Lippmann said as he wrote about *The Good Society:* "They have seen truly that the religious experience must forever raise up new enemies of the totalitarian state. For in that experience the convictions which the dictators must crush are bred and continually renewed."[25]

This ultimate loyalty must be kept alive in churches and families. That is the import of the fourth and fifth commandments. There are, in fact, no other organizations in our civilization than the Jewish synagogues (meeting according to the fourth commandment on the sabbath day) and the Christian churches (meeting in a way derived therefrom on the Lord's day), whose primary purpose it is to keep alive the moral and spiritual principles which the Decalogue represents. There is also little hope that even these can continue unless a respect for our moral and spiritual inheritance is transmitted through families, whose existence depends upon the teaching of the fifth commandment.

This ultimate loyalty must also guide and determine the relations of men to one another. If there were no God and if people were only machines or organisms, there would be no reason to respect human life. But since God is the Creator of all and has made man in his own image, we derive the positive principle of a genuine valuation of persons and perceive the necessity for protection of life, marriage, property, and social honor, as inculcated in the sixth to tenth commandments.

The Ten Commandments provide not only a lasting foundation for all community, but also an enduring structure for the guidance of personal life. Here, too, we may need to state the commandments positively as well as negatively, and try to understand the principles they embody. When we do, we find time-tested guidance as to the way of life which agrees with how things are in this universe under God. In his work of personal counseling, doubtless almost every pastor deals with persons who, taken together, have broken all of these commandments, and it is safe to say that almost every such person has in some manner and degree been broken upon the commandment which he has thought to flout. Perhaps by using the word "laws" for the commandments we even give a somewhat wrong impression. The Hebrew word *torah*, which was translated into the Greek of the Septuagint as *nomos* and hence came to us as "law," really means more than we usually understand by that word. As André Neher puts it: "The Hebrew word *Torah* does not signify order but orientation. It is not a Law, it is the way, the road along which a common enterprise is possible."[26] It is also, we are adding at this point, the way along which a personal enterprise is possible. Insofar as the Ten Commandments state fundamental principles which are in accord with the underlying structure of life, we do not get beyond them.

The abiding importance of these "ten rules for living" may be suggested by a story Clovis G. Chappell tells in a book of that name. Years ago a certain master and slave went deep-sea fishing. When they were coming back toward the shore late in the night, the master became sleepy and entrusted the helm to his faithful servant. But before doing so, he pointed out the north star to the man and urged him to keep his eye on it. Ere long, however, the servant, too, snatched forty winks. When he awakened he was in complete confusion. He called his master frantically. "Wake up!" he cried, "and show me another star. I've run past that one!"[27] In fact, however, we never run past the stars, nor, it seems, do we ever reach

the point where the principles grasped by Moses in the form of the
Ten Commandments lose their relevance.

Finally, the Ten Commandments suggest implications which
reach beyond their own literal words, inasmuch as they point to
more inward and less obvious matters. As to inwardness, it must always be remembered that the tenth commandment itself has to do
with desire, that is, with the inner direction of thought and purpose.
So Jesus was to go on in his own exposition of the inner meaning
of the Ten Commandments to show that the prohibition of murder
also implies the overcoming of anger: "You have heard that it was
said to the men of old, 'You shall not kill'. . . . But I say to you that
every one who is angry with his brother shall be liable to judgment. . . ." (Matthew 5:21-22). As to the implications of the Ten
Commandments relative to less obvious matters, we may think of
the words: "You shall not steal." Perhaps we have never committed robbery in the literal sense, but have we never taken away
from another person his chance to say what he wants to say by our
own impetuous talk, or stolen time another person needs by being
late to an appointment? Or: "You shall not bear false witness." Perhaps we have never committed perjury, but have we never circu-
lated some deleterious report or spoken contemptuous, malicious, or
unfair words?

So it is that the Ten Commandments provide permanent foundations of community and personal life and at least point, from their
own time and place, toward the teachings of the one who, many
years later, said that he had come not to destroy the law but to
fulfill it (Matthew 5:17). Plain in original formulation, and simple
in a modern children's version, the Ten Commandments continue
to speak with the accents of the divine authority in which Moses
first heard them:

> Above all else love God alone;
> Bow down to neither wood nor stone.
> God's name refuse to take in vain;
> The Sabbath rest with care maintain.
> Respect your parents all your days;
> Hold sacred human life always.
> Be loyal to your chosen mate;
> Steal nothing, neither small nor great.
> Report, with truth, your neighbor's deed;
> And rid your mind of selfish greed.[28]

# NOTES

## Abbreviations

| | |
|---|---|
| ASV | American Standard Version. |
| ANET | Ancient Near Eastern Texts Relating to the Old Testament, ed. by James B. Pritchard (Princeton: Princeton University Press, 2d ed. 1955). |
| ARAB | Ancient Records of Assyria and Babylonia, by Daniel D. Luckenbill (Chicago: The University of Chicago Press, 2 vols., 1926-27). |
| ARE | Ancient Records of Egypt, by James Henry Breasted (Chicago: The University of Chicago Press, 5 vols., 1906-07). |
| HDB | A Dictionary of the Bible, ed. by James Hastings (New York: Charles Scribner's Sons, 4 vols., 1898-1902). |
| IB | The Interpreter's Bible (New York and Nashville: Abingdon Press, 12 vols., 1952-57). |
| JAOS | Journal of the American Oriental Society. |
| JEA | The Journal of Egyptian Archaeology. |
| JNES | Journal of Near Eastern Studies. |
| KJV | King James Version. |
| Moffatt | The Old Testament, A New Translation by James Moffatt (New York: Harper & Brothers, 1924-25). |
| Pauly-Wissowa | Paulys Realencyclopädie der classischen Altertumswissenschaft, Neue Bearbeitung begonnen von Georg Wissowa, fortgeführt von Wilhelm Kroll und Karl Mittelhaus unter Mitwirkung zahlreicher Fachgenossen herausgegeben von Konrat Ziegler (Stuttgart: J. B. Metzlerscher Verlag, 1894 ff.; Alfred Druckenmüller Verlag, 1937 ff.). |
| RB | Revue Biblique. |
| RSV | Revised Standard Version. |
| SGTT | J. Simons, The Geographical and Topographical Texts of the Old Testament (Leiden: E. J. Brill, 1959). |

131

Preface

1. James Muilenburg, *The Way of Israel* (New York: Harper & Brothers, 1961), p. 49.

2. Further illustration of this point comes in the publication (after my own manuscript was completed) of *Let My People Go*, by Albert Luthuli (New York: McGraw-Hill, 1962), in which under this very title the Nobel Prize winner tells of his nonviolent resistance to oppression on behalf of his exploited people in South Africa.

Chapter 1.   The House of Bondage

1. ARE III, pp. 6-7.

2. ARE III, pp. 272-273; ANET p. 259.

3. ARE I, §493; ANET p. 19.

4. Carl Küthmann, *Die Ostgrenze Ägyptens* (Leipzig: W. Drugulin, 1911), p. 37.

5. Georg Ebers, *Durch Gosen zum Sinai* (Leipzig: Wilhelm Engelmann, 1872), pp. 471-473, and especially p. 473 for the identification of Sesostris.

6. ARE II, §292.

7. ARE II, §285.

8. ARE II, §§254, 263, 265.

9. ARE II, §§248, 266.

10. Roland G. Kent in JNES 1 (1942), p. 419; A. T. Olmstead, *History of the Persian Empire* (Chicago: The University of Chicago Press, 1948), p. 146.

11. C. Bourdon in RB 41 (1932), p. 371.

12. Karl Baedeker, *Egypt and the Sûdân* (Leipzig: Karl Baedeker, 7th ed. 1914), p. 180.

13. Fritz Hommel, *Ethnologie und Geographie des alten Orients* (Handbuch der Altertumswissenschaft III, i, 1) (München: C. H. Beck, 1926), p. 752.

14. *Ibid.*, p. 912.

15. *Ibid.*, pp. 978-981.

16. Ptolemy, Geography IV, 5, 53; Pauly-Wissowa 19:2, cols. 1611-1612.

17. ARE IV, §878.

18. ARAB II, §771; ANET p. 294.

19. Edouard Naville, *The Shrine of Saft el Henneh and the Land of Goshen* (London: Trübner & Co., 1887).

20. *Ibid.*, pp. 9, 16.

21. Hommel, *Ethnologie und Geographie des alten Orients*, pp. 973 ff.

22. Edouard Naville, *Bubastis* (London: Kegan Paul, Trench, Trübner & Co., 1891).

23. E. A. Wallis Budge, *The Gods of the Egyptians* (London: Methuen & Co., 1904), I, pp. 100, 498-499.

24. For Sopd as "the lord of the East" at Per-Sopd see Naville, *The*

*Shrine of Saft el Henneh and the Land of Goshen,* pp. 6 ff.; at Tell el-Maskhuta see Naville, *The Store-City of Pithom and the Route of the Exodus* (cited fully below in note 39), p. 16; and at Wadi Maghara see ARE I, §722.

25. Adolf Erman, *Die Ägyptische Religion* (Berlin: Georg Reimer, 1905), p. 21.

26. ARE I, §250; Küthmann, *Die Ostgrenze Ägyptens,* pp. 29-30.

27. ARE I, §§715, 722; Pierre Montet, *Everyday Life in Egypt* (New York: St. Martin's Press Inc., 1958), p. 142.

28. Hommel, *Ethnologie und Geographie des alten Orients,* pp. 916-920.

29. ARE I, §174.

30. Küthmann, *Die Ostgrenze Ägyptens,* p. 28.

31. ANET p. 3.

32. ARE III, §100.

33. Küthmann, *Die Ostgrenze Ägyptens,* p. 30.

34. See Alan H. Gardiner, "Sketch Map of the Eastern Delta," in JEA 5 (1918), Pl. XXXV facing p. 244; cf. Hommel, *Ethnologie und Geographie des alten Orients,* p. 915 note 4.

35. Gardiner in JEA 5 (1918), p. 262.

36. ANET p. 35.

37. Gardiner in JEA 5 (1918), p. 268.

38. ARE II, §§91, 189, 222; IV, §§183, 248.

39. Edouard Naville, *The Store-City of Pithom and the Route of the Exodus* (London: Trübner & Co., 1888).

40. *Ibid.,* p. 21 and Plate XI.

41. Gardiner in JEA 5 (1918), p. 269.

42. W. M. Flinders Petrie, *Hyksos and Israelite Cities* (London: School of Archaeology, 1906), pp. 28-34.

43. *Ibid.,* pp. 29, 31 and Plates XXIX, XXX.

44. Gardiner in JEA 5 (1918), p. 266.

45. Petrie, *Hyksos and Israelite Cities,* p. 31 and Plate XXXII.

46. Naville, *The Store-City of Pithom and the Route of the Exodus,* pp. 15-21; Gardiner in JEA 5 (1918), p. 268.

47. Georg Steindorff, "Die keilschriftliche Widergabe ägyptischer Eigennamen," in *Beiträge zur Assyriologie und vergleichenden semitischen Sprachwissenschaft,* ed. by Friedrich Delitzsch and Paul Haupt (Leipzig: J. C. Hinrichs), 1 (1890), p. 603; *A Hebrew and English Lexicon of the Old Testament,* by Francis Brown, S. R. Driver, and Charles A. Briggs (Oxford: Clarendon Press, 1957), p. 697.

48. H. Cazelles, "Les localisations de l'Exode," in RB 62 (1955), p. 357.

49. Samuel A. B. Mercer, *The Pyramid Texts* (New York, London, Toronto: Longmans, Green and Co., 1952), Line 628b (vol. I, p. 125; vol. II, p. 307); Küthmann, *Die Ostgrenze Ägyptens,* p. 33 note 3.

50. C. Bourdon, "La Route de l'Exode," in RB 41 (1932), pp. 373-374.

51. ANET pp. 19, 446.

52. Josephus, *Antiquities* II, 204 ( = II, ix, 1); *War* V, 382 ( = V, ix, 4).

53. *Antiquities* II, 318 ( = II, xv, 2).

54. John A. Wilson, *The Burden of Egypt* (Chicago: The University of Chicago Press, 1951), p. viii.

55. ARE II, §7.

56. J. Vergote, *Joseph en Égypte* (Louvain: Publications Universitaires, 1959). Joseph is placed under Amenhotep III by Z. Mayani, *Les Hyksos et le Monde de la Bible* (Paris: Payot, 1956); cf. Otto Eissfeldt in *Orientalistische Literaturzeitung* 1958 No. 7/8, col. 328; and under Amenhotep IV by H. H. Rowley, *Israel's Sojourn in Egypt* (Manchester: The Manchester University Press, 1938); and in *Journal of Semitic Studies* 5 (1960), p. 83.

57. Quoted by Martin Noth, *The History of Israel* (London: Adam & Charles Black, 2d ed. 1960), p. 113.

58. Diodorus I, 56, quoted in F. de Lanoye, *Rameses the Great; or, Egypt 3300 Years Ago* (New York: Scribner, 1872), p. 163.

59. Josephus, *Antiquities* II, 204 (= II, ix, 1).

60. Gerhard von Rad, *Moses* (World Christian Books 32) (London: Lutterworth Press, 1960), pp. 8-9.

## Chapter 2.   Pharaoh and Moses

1. ARE III, §285.

2. Richard A. Parker in JNES 16 (1957), pp. 39-43.

3. M. B. Rowton in *Journal of Cuneiform Studies* 13 (1959), pp. 8-9; JNES 19 (1960), pp. 15-22.

4. Pierre Montet, *L'Égypte et la Bible* (Neuchatel: Éditions Delachaux & Niestlé, 1959), p. 29.

5. John A. Wilson, *The Burden of Egypt* (Chicago: The University of Chicago Press, 1951), pp. 245-251.

6. *Ibid.*, p. 252.

7. *The Encyclopaedia Britannica*, 14th ed. (1929), vol. 13, p. 283.

8. *The National Geographic Magazine* 80 (1941), pp. 473, 513.

9. Nancy Grace in *Harper's Bazaar*, November 1960, pp. 96, 100; see also *Horizon*, July 1960.

10. ANET p. 231.

11. Mercer, *The Pyramid Texts*, Lines 218d-e-f (vol. I, p. 69; vol. II, p. 102).

12. ANET p. 231, cf. p. 249.

13. ANET p. 252.

14. Budge, *The Gods of the Egyptians*, II, pp. 243-244.

15. Karl Baedeker, *Ägypten und der Sûdân* (Leipzig: Karl Baedeker, 8th ed. 1928), p. 124.

16. Hommel, *Ethnologie und Geographie des alten Orients*, p. 962.

17. ARE II, §§4-12.

18. Manetho, ed. W. G. Waddell (Loeb Classical Library), pp. 80-83, 86-87, 124-125.

19. ARE III, §261.

20. ARE III, §371; ANET p. 199.

21. ARE III, §406.

22. Alan H. Gardiner in JEA 3 (1916), p. 101; 5 (1918), p. 246.

23. Gardiner in JEA 5 (1918), pp. 199-200, 248.
24. ANET p. 26; Gardiner in JEA 5 (1918), p. 248.
25. Manetho, ed. Waddell, pp. 154-155.
26. ARAB II, §§771, 844.
27. Pierre Montet in RB 39 (1930), p. 8.
28. *The Encyclopaedia Britannica*, 14th ed. (1929), vol. 19, p. 863.
29. Manetho, ed. Waddell, pp. 80-81.
30. Hommel, *Ethnologie und Geographie des alten Orients*, p. 902.
31. Montet in RB 39 (1930), pp. 15-18.
32. ARE I, §165.
33. Küthmann, *Die Ostgrenze Ägyptens*, pp. 43-44.
34. Gardiner in JEA 5 (1918), pp. 242-244; 6 (1920), p. 104.
35. Gardiner in JEA 5 (1918), pp. 247-249; 19 (1933), p. 126.
36. Gardiner in JEA 5 (1918), p. 251.
37. Gardiner in JEA 5 (1918), pp. 185-186; ANET p. 471.
38. Gardiner in JEA 19 (1933), p. 126.
39. Raymond Weill in JEA 21 (1935), pp. 21-22.
40. Pierre Montet in *Syria* 17 (1936), p. 200.
41. Weill in JEA 21 (1935), p. 10 and note 1.
42. W. M. Flinders Petrie, *Tanis*, Parts I and II (Second and Fourth Memoirs of the Egypt Exploration Fund) (London: Trübner & Co., 1888-89).
43. *The Egyptian Museum, Cairo, A Brief Description of the Principal Monuments* (Cairo: Government Press, 1956), p. 37, No. 507.
44. *Ibid.*, p. 39, Nos. 613, 617; Petrie, *Tanis*, Part I, Pl. III, No. 17; Part II, p. 18, No. 17.
45. Petrie, *Tanis*, Part I, Pl. II, No. 5; Part II, p. 16, No. 5.
46. Weill in JEA 21 (1935), p. 10.
47. Petrie, *Tanis*, Part II, Pl. II, Nos. 76, 77, 78; ARE III, §§487-491.
48. Petrie, *Tanis*, Part I, Pls. VII-XI; ARE III, p. 228, note c.
49. ARE III, §§538-542; ANET pp. 252-253; Weill in JEA 21 (1935), pp. 19-21.
50. Pierre Montet, *Les nouvelles fouilles de Tanis (1929-1932)* (Paris: Les Belles Lettres, 1933); *Le Drame d'Avaris* (1941); *Tanis, douze années de fouilles dans une capitale oubliée du delta égyptien* (Paris: Payot, 1942); *Les enigmes de Tanis* (Paris: Payot, 1952); *Géographie de l'Égypte ancienne*, Part I (Paris: Imprimerie Nationale, 1957), pp. 192-203; and articles in *Kêmi, Revue de philologie et d'archéologie égyptiennes et coptes* (Paris: Librairie Orientaliste Paul Geuthner).
51. Weill in JEA 21 (1935), pp. 12-13.
52. Gardiner in JEA 19 (1933), p. 127.
53. Montet, *L'Égypte et la Bible*, pp. 53-54.
54. Gardiner in JEA 19 (1933), p. 126.
55. Montet in RB 39 (1930), p. 14; *Les nouvelles fouilles de Tanis (1929-1932)*, pp. 110-112, Pls. LVII-LVIII.
56. Montet, *L'Égypte et la Bible*, pp. 53-54.
57. Mahmud Hamza in *Annales du service des antiquites de l'Égypte* 30 (1930), pp. 31-68.
58. B. Couroyer in RB 53 (1946), pp. 75-98.

59. Albrecht Ält in *Festschrift für Friedrich Zucker* (Berlin: Akademie Verlag, 1954), pp. 3-13.

60. Gardiner in JEA 5 (1918), pp. 185-187; ANET pp. 470-471.

61. Wilson, *The Burden of Egypt*, p. 252.

62. André Neher, *Moïse* (Collection "Maitres Spirituels") (Paris: Editions du Seuil); *Moses and the Vocation of the Jewish People* (New York and Evanston: Harper & Row; London: Longmans, Green & Co. Ltd., Men of Wisdom paperback series, 1959), pp. 73, 75.

63. Eduard Meyer, *Die Israeliten und ihre Nachbarstämme* (Halle a. S.: Verlag von Max Niemeyer, 1906), p. 415, note 1.

64. Martin Noth, *The History of Israel* (London: Adam & Charles Black, 2d ed. 1960), p. 136.

65. Henry S. Noerdlinger, *Moses and Egypt* (Los Angeles: University of Southern California Press, 1956), pp. 18-19. On the attempt to find direct references to Moses in Egyptian sources, see Rudolf Smend, *Das Mosebild von Heinrich Ewald bis Martin Noth* (Beiträge zur Geschichte der biblischen Exegese, 3) (Tübingen: J. C. B. Mohr [Paul Siebeck]), pp. 23-25.

66. W. F. Albright, *The Archaeology of Palestine* (Harmondsworth, Middlesex: Penguin Books Limited, 1949), p. 224.

67. G. Steindorff in Baedeker, *Ägypten*, 8th ed. 1928, pp. CXXXVII, CXXXIX; *Egypt*, 7th ed. 1914, pp. cxxxii, cxxxiv; Alan H. Gardiner in JAOS 56 (1936), p. 192.

68. ANET pp. 448, 475.

69. J. Gwyn Griffiths in JNES 12 (1953), pp. 225-231.

70. Gardiner in JAOS 56 (1936), pp. 192-195; Theophile J. Meek in *The American Journal of Semitic Languages and Literatures* 56 (1939), pp. 118-119; Griffiths in JNES 12 (1953), p. 230, note 65.

71. W. F. Albright in JAOS 74 (1954), pp. 229, 233.

72. John Bright, *A History of Israel* (Philadelphia: The Westminster Press, 1959), p. 116.

73. Yehezkel Kaufmann, *The Religion of Israel* (Chicago: The University of Chicago Press, 1960), p. 224.

74. *Cf.* Midrash Rabbah, *Exodus* (Beshallach), XX, 19 (London: Soncino Press, 1939), p. 258 and note 5.

75. Midrash Rabbah, *Exodus* (Shemoth), I, 26, Soncino ed. p. 34.

76. *Ibid.*, I, 27, Soncino ed. p. 34.

77. *Ibid.*, V, 2, Soncino ed. p. 82.

78. Adolf Erman, *Life in Ancient Egypt* (London: Macmillan & Co., 1894), p. 48.

79. Wilson, *The Burden of Egypt*, p. 253.

## Chapter 3. The Plagues of Egypt

1. Eduard Meyer, *Die Israeliten und ihre Nachbarstämme* (Halle a. S.: Verlag von Max Niemeyer, 1906), p. 31.

2. J. Coert Rylaarsdam in IB 1, pp. 838-839.

3. Daniel P. Mannix in *Holiday*, November 1960, p. 32.

4. Samuel A. B. Mercer, *The Pyramid Texts* (New York, London, Toronto: Longmans, Green and Co., 1952), Line 564a (vol. IV, p. 65).

5. ANET p. 372.
6. Mercer, *The Pyramid Texts*, vol. II, p. 85.
7. W. E. Crum in HDB III, p. 550.
8. Melvin G. Kyle, *Moses and the Monuments* (Oberlin, Ohio: Bibliotheca Sacra Company, 1920), p. 49.
9. Greta Hort in *Zeitschrift für die alttestamentliche Wissenschaft* 69 (1957), pp. 84-103; 70 (1958), pp. 48-59.
10. *Ibid.*, 69 (1957), p. 84, note.
11. Gessner, *Hydrobotanik* (Berlin, 1955), vol. I, pp. 412-413; cited by Hort, *op. cit.*, 69 (1957), p. 94.
12. S. R. Driver, *The Book of Exodus* (The Cambridge Bible for Schools and Colleges) (Cambridge: The University Press, 1911), p. 65, note 1.
13. *Cf.* Martin Buber, *Moses* (Oxford and London: East and West Library, published by Phaidon Press Ltd., Oxford, 1946), p. 68.
14. Hort, *op. cit.*, 70 (1958), pp. 58-59.
15. *Cf.* Paul Volz, *Prophetengestalten des Alten Testaments* (Stuttgart: Calwer Verlag, 1949).
16. Buber, *Moses*, p. 64.
17. Rylaarsdam in IB 1, p. 839.

### Chapter 4. Let My People Go

1. Rudolf Kittel, *Geschichte des Volkes Israel* (Stuttgart: W. Kohlhammer), vol. 1, 7th ed. 1932, p. 341 and note 3, pp. 365-366.
2. Martin Noth, *The History of Israel* (London: Adam & Charles Black, 2d ed. 1960), pp. 117, 136 and note 2.
3. J. Coert Rylaarsdam in IB 1, pp. 836, 839.
4. Bernhard W. Anderson, *Understanding the Old Testament* (Englewood Cliffs, N. J.: Prentice-Hall, Inc., 1957), pp. 40, 42, 44.
5. Rylaarsdam in IB 1, p. 847.
6. André Neher, *Moïse* (Collection "Maitres Spirituels") (Paris: Éditions du Seuil); English translation, *Moses and the Vocation of the Jewish People* (New York and Evanston: Harper & Row; London: Longmans, Green & Co. Ltd., Men of Wisdom, paperback series, 1959), p. 90.
7. *Ibid.*, pp. 27-28. Quoted by permission of Éditions du Seuil, Paris, and Longmans, Green & Co. Ltd., London.
8. James Parkes, *A History of Palestine from 135 A.D. to Modern Times* (New York: Oxford University Press, 1949), pp. 180-181.
9. Leon Uris, *Exodus* (Garden City, N. Y.: Doubleday and Company, Inc., 1958).

### Chapter 5. Passover!

1. William Robertson Smith, *The Religion of the Semites* (New York: The Macmillan Company, 3d ed. 1927), pp. 227, 641 f.
2. Antonin Jaussen, *Coutumes des Arabes au pays de Moab* (Paris: Librairie Victor Lecoffe, J. Gabalda & Cie., 1908), pp. 366-367.
3. John Lewis Burckhardt, *Notes on the Bedouins and Wahábys* (London: Henry Colburn and Richard Bentley, 1830), p. 33.

4. Samuel I. Curtiss, *Primitive Semitic Religion To-day* (New York: Fleming H. Revell Company, 1902), pp. 183, 187.

5. Xenophon, *Anabasis* I, iv, 11, 17.

6. *Cf. The Berkeley Version* (Grand Rapids, Michigan: Zondervan Publishing House, 2d ed. 1959), p. 711, note q.

7. Martin Buber, *Moses* (London: East and West Library, 1946), pp. 69-70. Quoted by permission.

8. Amran Ishak, *The History and Religion of the Samaritans* (Jerusalem: Greek Convent Press), pp. 5-6; *The Commandments of the Samaritans on Mount Gerizim*, by the Tribe of the Samaritans, Priests in Nablus (Jerusalem: Greek Convent Press), pp. 4-9.

9. A. H. McNeile, *The Book of Exodus* (Westminster Commentaries) (New York: Edwin S. Gorham; London: Methuen & Co., 1908), p. 64.

10. The Mishnah, Pesahim 5, 5-7, ed. Herbert Danby (Oxford University Press; London: Humphrey Milford, 1933), p. 142.

11. *Form of Service for the Two First Nights of the Feast of Passover* (New York: L. H. Frank, 1869=5629); Theodor H. Gaster, *Passover* (New York: Henry Schuman, 1949); *Festivals of the Jewish Year* (New York: William Sloane Associates, 1952, 1953), pp. 31-58.

12. Gaster, *Festivals of the Jewish Year*, p. 42.

13. *Ibid.*, p. 32.

### Chapter 6.  Through the Sea

1. Martin Noth, *The History of Israel* (London: Adam & Charles Black, 2d ed. 1960), pp. 115, 116, 117.

2. Josephus, *War* IV, 661-662 (=IV, xi, 5).

3. F.-M. Abel, *Géographie de la Palestine* (Paris: J. Gabalda et Cie., 2 vols. 1933-1938), II, p. 218.

4. Alan H. Gardiner in JEA 6 (1920), pp. 99-116, and, for the quotations, see specially pp. 101, 116. See also Alan H. Gardiner, *Egypt of the Pharaohs* (Oxford: Clarendon Press, 1961), p. 253.

5. Otto Eissfeldt, *Baal Zaphon, Zeus Kasios und der Durchzug der Israeliten durches Meer* (Beiträge zur Religionsgeschichte des Altertums, 1) (Halle [Saale]: Max Niemeyer Verlag, 1932).

6. Georg Beer, *Exodus* (Handbuch zum Alten Testament) (Tübingen: J. C. B. Mohr [Paul Siebeck], 1939), p. 75.

7. H. Cazelles in RB 62 (1955), pp. 321-364.

8. Martin Noth in *Festschrift Otto Eissfeldt* (Halle an der Saale: Max Niemeyer, 1947), pp. 181-190; *The History of Israel* (2d ed. 1960), pp. 115-116.

9. Eissfeldt, *Baal Zaphon, Zeus Kasios und der Durchzug der Israeliten durches Meer*, pp. 40f.

10. Cazelles in RB 62 (1955), pp. 332-336.

11. Eissfeldt, *op. cit.*, pp. 66 f.

12. Cazelles in RB 62 (1955), pp. 336-337.

13. ANET pp. 249 f.

14. SGTT p. 247, note 211.

15. C. Bourdon in RB 41 (1932), pp. 373-374.

16. *Ibid.*, p. 376, Fig. 2.

17. Cazelles in RB 62 (1955), p. 358.
18. SGTT pp. 242, 247.
19. C. Bourdon in RB 37 (1928), p. 234, Fig. 1.
20. Bourdon in RB 41 (1932), pp. 378-390.
21. Bourdon in RB 37 (1928), p. 234, Fig. 1; p. 243, Fig. 3.
22. SGTT p. 250.
23. Joseph Offord in *Palestine Exploration Fund Quarterly Statement* for 1919, pp. 175-177.
24. SGTT p. 248.
25. HDB III, p. 367.
26. Abel, *Géographie de la Palestine* II, p. 208; SGTT p. 249.
27. ANET p. 471 and note 17.
28. SGTT p. 237.
29. J. Coert Rylaarsdam in IB 1, p. 938.
30. James H. Breasted, *A History of Egypt* (New York: Charles Scribner's Sons, 1905), Fig. 170 facing p. 464; André Neher, *Moses and the Vocation of the Jewish People* (New York and Evanston: Harper & Row; London: Longmans, Green & Co. Ltd., Men of Wisdom paperback series, 1959), Fig. on p. 68; Pierre Montet, *L'Égypte et la Bible* (Neuchatel: Éditions Delachaux & Niestlé, 1959), Pl. I facing p. 16.
31. Martin Buber, *Moses* (London: East and West Library, 1946), pp. 75-77.

## Chapter 7. From Egypt to Sinai

1. Josephus, *War* II, 385 (=II, xvi, 4).
2. Georg Beer, *Exodus* (Handbuch zum Alten Testament) (Tübingen: J. C. B. Mohr [Paul Siebeck], 1939), p. 69.
3. *Ibid.*
4. W. M. Flinders Petrie, *Egypt and Israel* (London: Society for Promoting Christian Knowledge, new ed. 1923), p. 44.
5. George E. Mendenhall in *Journal of Biblical Literature* 77 (1958), pp. 52-66.
6. James G. Murphy, *A Critical and Exegetical Commentary on the Book of Exodus* (Andover: Warren F. Draper; Boston: W. H. Halliday and Company, 1868), p. 136; A. H. McNeile, *The Book of Exodus* (Westminster Commentaries) (New York: Edwin S. Gorham; London: Methuen & Co., 1908), p. 81; Beer, *Exodus*, p. 74.
7. Midrash Rabbah, *Numbers* (Bemidbar), II, 7 (London: Soncino Press, 1939), Numbers I, pp. 28-30.
8. James H. Breasted, *A History of Egypt* (New York: Charles Scribner's Sons, 1905), p. 30; Adolf Erman, *Life in Ancient Egypt* (London: Macmillan and Co., 1894), pp. 546-547.
9. McNeile, *The Book of Exodus*, p. 82.
10. For the identifications of the sites see F. -M. Abel, *Géographie de la Palestine* (Paris: J. Gabalda et Cie., 2 vols. 1933-1938), II, pp. 210-213; SGTT pp. 251-253; L. H. Grollenberg, *Atlas of the Bible* (New York, London, etc.: Thomas Nelson and Sons, 1956), Map 9.
11. Abel, *Géographie de la Palestine*, I, p. 391.

12. Georg Ebers, *Durch Gosen zum Sinai* (Leipzig: Wilhelm Engelmann, 1872), Map facing p. 108.

13. Beer, *Exodus*, p. 97.

14. Martin Noth, *Das zweite Buch Mose, Exodus* (Das Alte Testament Deutsch) (Göttingen: Vandenhoeck & Ruprecht, 1959), p. 124.

15. Ebers, *Durch Gosen zum Sinai*, p. 117.

16. Ferdinand de Lesseps, *L'isthme de Suez* (Paris 1864), p. 10, cited by Ebers, *Durch Gosen zum Sinai*, p. 117 and p. 531, note 77.

17. Emil G. Kraeling, *Rand McNally Bible Atlas* (Chicago: Rand McNally & Company, 1956), p. 108.

18. McNeile, *The Book of Exodus*, p. 97.

19. Marston Bates in *The American Scholar* 29 (1959-60), pp. 46-48.

## Chapter 8. Moses and Monotheism

1. Robert H. Pfeiffer, *Religion in the Old Testament* (New York: Harper & Brothers, 1961), pp. 49, 54, 141.

2. H. and H. A. Frankfort, John A. Wilson, Thorkild Jacobsen, and William A. Irwin, *The Intellectual Adventure of Ancient Man* (Chicago: The University of Chicago Press, 1946); H. and H. A. Frankfort, John A. Wilson, and Thorkild Jacobsen, *Before Philosophy* (Harmondsworth, Middlesex: Penguin Books Ltd., 1949).

3. For the religion of ancient Egypt see E. A. Wallis Budge, *The Gods of the Egyptians* (London: Methuen & Co., 2 vols. 1904); Adolf Erman, *Die Ägyptische Religion* (Berlin: Georg Reimer, 1905); H. Frankfort, *Ancient Egyptian Religion* (New York: Columbia University Press, 1948).

4. ANET p. 370.

5. Karl Baedeker, *Egypt and the Sûdân* (Leipzig: Karl Baedeker, 7th ed. 1914), p. 344.

6. Budge, *The Gods of the Egyptians*, I, pp. 294, 356.

7. Frankfort, *Ancient Egyptian Religion*, pp. 13, 23.

8. *Ibid.*, p. 24.

9. *Ibid.*, p. 25.

10. *Ibid.*, p. 11.

11. Erman, *Die Ägyptische Religion*, p. 164.

12. Josephus, *Antiquities* II, 227 (=II, ix, 5).

13. *Ibid.*, 257 (=II, xi, 1).

14. S. R. Driver, *The Book of Exodus* (The Cambridge Bible) (Cambridge: University Press, 1911), p. 14.

15. Martin Buber, *Moses* (London: East and West Library, 1946), p. 41.

16. *Ibid.*, p. 48.

17. *Cf. ibid.*, pp. 52 f.; Raymond Abba, "The Divine Name Yahweh," in *Journal of Biblical Literature* 80 (1961), pp. 320-328.

18. *The Intellectual Adventure of Ancient Man*, pp. 363.

19. Yehezkel Kaufmann, *The Religion of Israel* (Chicago: The University of Chicago Press, 1960), p. 121. For a critique of Kaufmann see J. Philip Hyatt in *The Journal of Bible and Religion* 29 (1961), pp. 52-57.

20. Kaufmann, *The Religion of Israel*, p. 227.

21. *Ibid.*, p. 225.

## Chapter 9. The Ten Commandments

1. Robert H. Pfeiffer, *Introduction to the Old Testament* (New York: Harper & Brothers, 5th ed. 1941), pp. 210-211.

2. *Cf.* J. Vergote, *Joseph en Égypte* (Louvain: Publications Universitaires, 1959), p. 210, note 2.

3. John A. Wilson in ANET p. 212.

4. ARE II, §433.

5. Yehezkel Kaufmann, *The Religion of Israel* (Chicago: The University of Chicago Press, 1960), p. 170.

6. ANET p. 163.

7. Robert F. Harper, *The Code of Hammurabi King of Babylon* (Chicago: The University of Chicago Press, 1904), p. 87.

8. G. R. Driver and John C. Miles, *The Babylonian Laws* (Oxford: Clarendon Press, 2 vols. 1952-55), I, p. 444.

9. Kaufmann, *The Religion of Israel*, p. 170.

10. *Ibid.*, p. 171; *cf.* F. C. Fensham, "The Possibility of the Presence of Casuistic Legal Material at the Making of the Covenant at Sinai," in *Palestine Exploration Quarterly*, Jul.-Dec. 1961, pp. 143-146.

11. Julius Wellhausen, *Prolegomena to the History of Israel* (Edinburgh: Adam & Charles Black, 1885), pp. 343, 393, 397 and note 1.

12. Karl Budde, *Religion of Israel to the Exile* (New York and London: G. P. Putnam's Sons, 1899), p. 32.

13. Georg Beer, *Exodus* (Handbuch zum Alten Testament) (Tübingen: J. C. B. Mohr [Paul Siebeck], 1939), p. 103.

14. J. J. Stamm, *Der Dekalog im Lichte der neueren Forschung* (Bern: Paul Haupt, 1958); Walter Beyerlin, *Herkunft und Geschichte der ältesten Sinaitraditionen* (Tübingen: J. C. B. Mohr, 1961).

15. Albrecht Alt, *Die Ursprünge des israelitischen Rechts* (Berichte über die Verhandlungen der Sächsischen Akademie der Wissenschaften zu Leipzig, Philologisch-historische Klasse, 86. Band. 1934. I. Heft) (Leipzig: S. Hirzel, 1934).

16. H. H. Rowley, *Moses and the Decalogue* (Manchester: Manchester University Press, 1951), pp. 101-102.

17. Martin Buber, *Moses* (London: East and West Library, 1946), p. 136.

18. *Ibid.*, p. 124.

19. Volz, *Mose*, 2d ed. 1932, p. 25, quoted by Buber, *ibid.*, p. 136.

20. Buber, *Moses*, pp. 139-140.

21. *Ibid.*, p. 133.

22. James G. Murphy, *A Critical and Exegetical Commentary on the Book of Exodus* (Andover: Warren F. Draper, 1868), p. 222.

23. Augustine, *The City of God*, I, 20.

24. Elton Trueblood, *Foundations for Reconstruction* (New York: Harper & Brothers, 1946, 1962), p. 10.

25. Walter Lippmann, *The Good Society* (Boston: Little, Brown and Company, 1937), p. 383; quoted by Trueblood, *op. cit.*, p. 14.

26. André Neher, *Moses and the Vocation of the Jewish People* (New

York and Evanston: Harper & Row; London: Longmans, Green & Co. Ltd., Men of Wisdom paperback series, 1959), p. 106.

27. Clovis G. Chappell, *Ten Rules for Living* (Nashville: Cokesbury Press, 1938), p. 12.

28. Trueblood, *Foundations for Reconstruction*, p. 10.

# Name and Subject Index

143

# Scripture Index

*Set in Linotype Caledonia*
*Composed, printed and bound by The Haddon Craftsmen, Inc.*
HARPER & ROW, PUBLISHERS, INCORPORATED